War And Bloodletting Under A Sick President

War And Bloodletting Under A Sick President

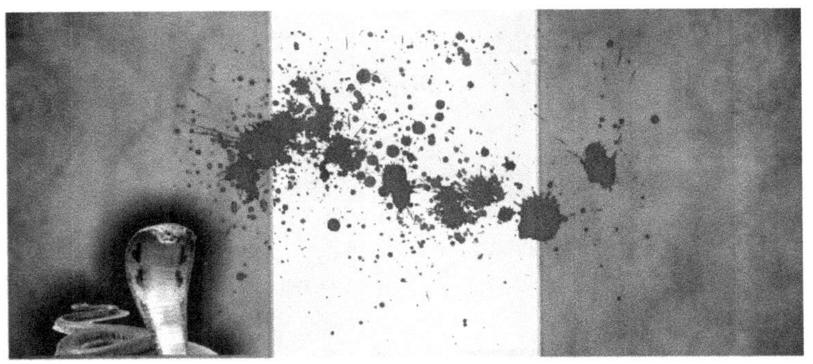

The Lamentation of
Ilenloa Igberaese

Published by Alowiz Publishers
Benin City, Nigeria

Printed in Nigeria by
Ethereal Publishing, Benin City

ISBN 987-987-54817-0-1

Suggested Reading Age: 16+
First Edition

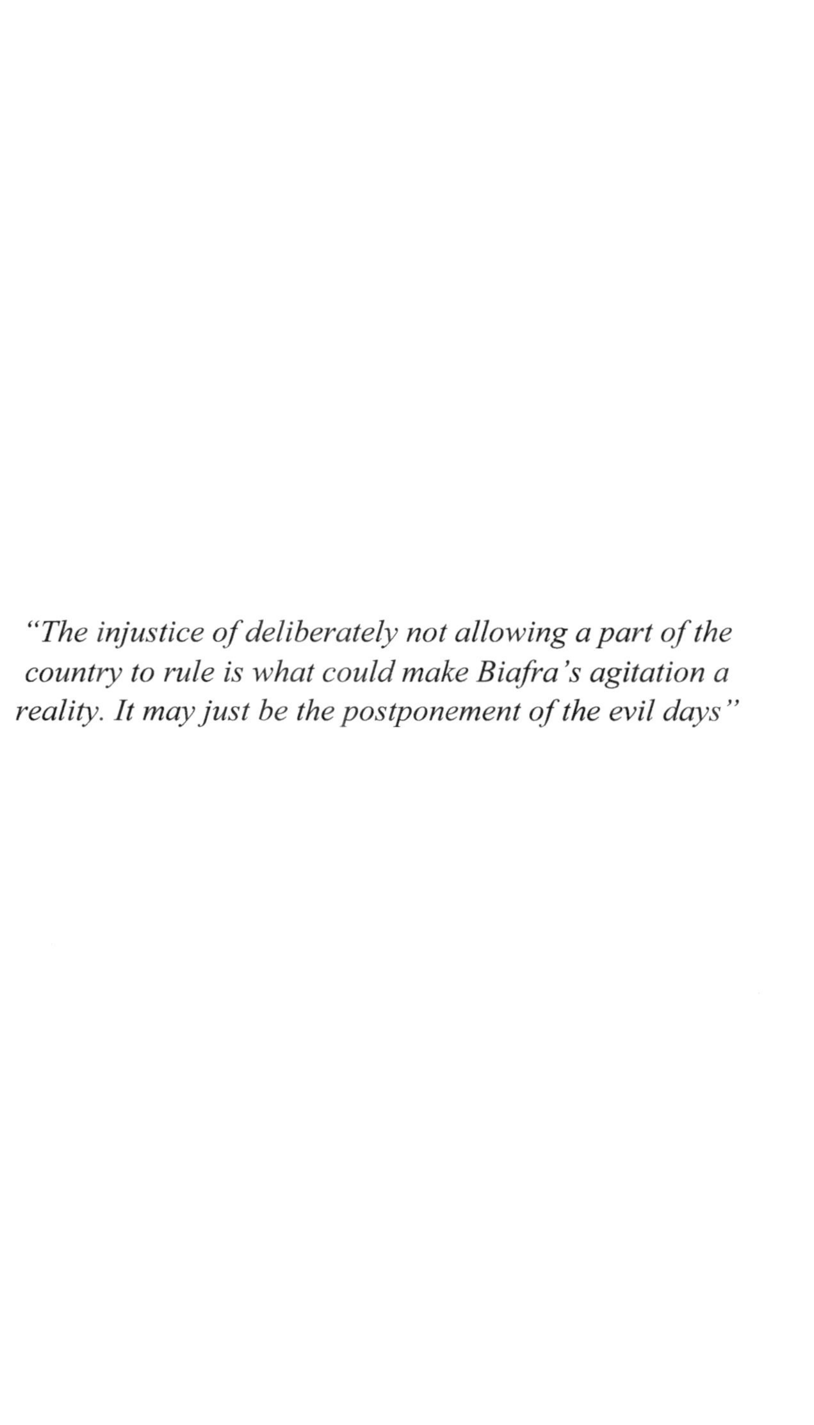

"The injustice of deliberately not allowing a part of the country to rule is what could make Biafra's agitation a reality. It may just be the postponement of the evil days"

Foreword

War and bloodletting under a sick president! What kind of a book title is this? Nevertheless, the author, Ilenloa Igberaese insists this title was given to him in a dream. I have no option than to come to terms with it; after all, as they say, the truth is always bitter. Yes! The book focuses a detailed attention on what we all know and have been talking about in parts; the untold suffering of the ordinary man and woman in Nigeria occasioned by the activities of the new Fulani herdsmen, which the author traces to the wrong decisions we all made with our thumbs in 2015, which we repeated in 2019.Please, note that I speak of the "new Fulani herdsmen" because in the past, we only knew herdsmen because they were very peaceful and friendly with their host communities. The author also highly acknowledges this fact throughout the book, and I am very happy that he does not give a blanket ill-fated impression of the Fulani and their leaders – the true Fulani and the non-true Fulani. Indeed, he has a lot of good advocacies for the poor Fulani people.

He says the purpose of his book is to enable the unborn generations know what we, who would become their past generation, went through in the hands of our leaders (not just one), when Nigeria would have finally become a good place to be born and live in; so that they may understand that it has not always been "the labour of our heroes past". I see that as great patriotism and hope for a better Nigeria. He preaches against sectionalism and bigotry in governance by being hard on the supporters of what he calls Buburism (please find this out for yourself). A critical reader will discover that. Igberaese spares nobody in his anger against leadership and societal evils in Nigeria; not even his much cherished academic profession, as he posits that even the Professor who takes undue advantage of, and deliberately makes life miserable for his students must die for his students to live. That includes himself, I suppose. He does not even spare his father, one of the late "Federal Soldiers" who he said only fought for his employment instead of his convictions during the civil war.

Someone should have thought that the author attempts to intimidate the rest of us who do not belong to the economics classification, but he says NO! He only attempts to look forward with what he knows best as they relate to the messages of his book. He is educated in economics to the highest level, specializes in an innovative area of Health Economics, which he combines with Development Economics. He teaches and practices economics in his daily life and as he has said to me, he is an oriental, not an accidental economist. Why then would he not purposefully bring his life to bear in talking to all of us? In his advocacies for youth development in Nigeria, policy frameworks for a better Nigeria, especially on the economy, education and health systems, he has demonstrated that schooling in Nigeria is not after all, as low a standard as I had thought. Indeed, the book is a painstaking effort and intensive in narration. It is well researched; a good resource materials for politicians of goodwill, public policy makers and also for the purpose of pedagogy in many disciplines.

I must warn that as interesting as the book is, it is a hard-read. I recommend that readers should develop the stamina to read through all the pages of the book, if they would not get the author's messages only in parts. However, if they find a page(s) of the book too difficult to read, they can jump that page(s), since the book is designed in such a way that readers can always connect to their areas of interest. For example, it took me great stamina to read the interesting biographies of some notable men like John Maynard Keynes, Jean-Baptiste Colbert and St. Thomas Aquinas, as well as the economic equations demonstrated in the book. If I had not bothered myself, I would have still rolled on. Despite this benevolent style of his, readers should actually not read the book in parts; otherwise they would get the language of the book wrong. In that case, they would internalize it in error and believe that the author is pro Igbo but anti-north or anti Fulani people, whereas the contrary is the case. He only attacks some evils of the elites, who subdue their people and capitalize on the ignorance for selfish interest. Imagine an author from southern part of the country advocating that the Central Bank of Nigeria should give grants or interest free loans to the poor Fulani herdsmen to establish ranches and declaring that they are vulnerable to attacks. Imagine him supporting the idea that the north feed the nation.

Like I said of the title, I do not, after all, agree with the whole of the author's position concerning his views of Nigeria and his judgments of the various leaders. I pointed some of my disagreements out to him but he insists that his lamentation and dreams are involuntary and unintentional but messages from God. Who then am I to dilute the messages, which an author has said that God had chosen only him at this time to deliver to his country people; the born and unborn generations? The book is divided into two parts. Part 1 is a mixed fiction, which is entirely of the author. Part 2 is a collation of the supposed lamentations in parts by Nigerians with brief comments of the author.

Finally, I envy and congratulate all those whose names appear on the honour page of the book, even though I do not know what the author mean by the coming holy books and how they would look like. I would have contended some names in the list but the criteria are only known to the author. Anyway, it shows that unknown angels are always there to watch over what we all do.

Anonymous

In no particular order.
In Honour of:

1. Mazi Nnamdi Kanu
2. Gov. Nyesom Wike
3. Bishop Matthew Hassan Kukah
4. Sen. Enyinnaya Abaribe
5. Prof. Chukwuma Soludo
6. Professor Pat Utomi
7. Otunba Sunday Igboho
8. Bishop David Oyedepo
9. Sen. Dino Melaye
10. Gov. Samuel Ortom
11. Gov. Godwin Obaseki – The money printing alarmist
12. Ex-Gov. Ayo Fayose
13. Ex-Gov. Olusegun Mimiko
14. Chief Mike Ozekhome, SAN
15. Prof. Wole Soyinka
16. Gov. Rotimi Akeredolu, SAN
17. Bishop Matthew Okpebholo – who often fix the government abandoned roads in my area
18. Prof. Jerry Gana
19. Chief Dan Osi Orbih
20. Sen. Shehu Sani
21. Gen. Olusegu Obasanjo, the letter writer
22. Apostle Johnson Suleman
23. Dr. Bukola Saraki
24. Femi Falana (SAN)
25. Marxist Kola Edokpayi
26. Mr. Peter Obi and all the Obi-dents
27. Sowere Omoyele – "Revolution Now"
28. The Afenife – The father of restructuring
29. The peaceful and non-violent Fulanis in Nigeria
30. ENDSARS Conveners, Leaders, Victims and Protesters

They have been courageous enough to speak truth to power. Their name would be written in the holy books to come.

Declaration

I hereby solemnly uphold the truth that I dreamt, and that I love my country Nigeria; to remain loyal to her, instead of any government in power that is not inspired to prosper the citizens and make the country proud in the comity of nations. I affirm that I do not write on my own but as the spirit leads, and that I write because Nigeria is the only country I have. So, help me, God.

Content

Part One

Chapter 1: General Introduction 1

Chapter 2: General Introduction Continued 19

Chapter 3: Once Great 29

Chapter 4: Political Bourgeoisie 34

Chapter 5: So Daft.................................... 42

Chapter 6: Like the Children of Israel................ 59

Chapter 7: Who Would Rescue Them?..................... 71

Chapter 8: President Mohammadu Baba Bubu's
  Supporters... 76

Chapter 9: My Short Presentation 83

Chapter 10: Before the First Century 97

Chapter 11: Such a Bigot 109

Chapter 12: This Love for Cows 116

Chapter 13: Overall Burden of Disease................. 131

Chapter 14: And the Problem Continues................. 142

Chapter 15: Upon Baba Bubu's Return................... 151

Part Two 159

Index 206

PART ONE

CHAPTER ONE

General Introduction

<u>Paranoia</u>

Perhaps my unceasing concerns for my country have triggered continuous and long daily dreams in me. Of course, dreams are involuntary of humans, from which I am not exempted. As a man who it has pleased God to originate in this part of the world called Nigeria, I initially feared to narrate my dreadful dreams; not even to my wife, because even the walls have ears to hear me and whisper to the President and his men.

I had to fear because as a student of the Bible from my infancy, I was told the story by my village catechist in the local Catholic Church, from where I began my Christian life, of how Joseph's narration of a mere dream to his brothers had landed him in trouble.

So, I FEAR
I feared that if I dare narrate my dreams
People would wonder how possible this was
They would call my claims mendacities
Forgetting that they did not even sleep in my small bed
Let alone being hypnotized to dream with me.

I feared that I might be beleaguered and careworn
Since selfish interests and benefits are unaided
Or when egos are not massaged
Forgetting how unscrupulous of them
To contend any dream with a dreamer.

I feared that for daring to narrate mere dreams
I may be harried in my dear country
Which I have served in all my youth-adult life
With more than a quarter spent in humanizing
Those on whose shoulders rest the next generations.

I feared that I may lose some of my Fulani friends
With whom I had done marvelous stuffs
The fellows may then easily believe
That I have hurled a blanket attack on their heritage
But no, it is not at all.

I fear that just a book is not enough for my dreams.
How big would it be?
Who would carry and read it?
All the pains I dreamt
That Baba Bubu has caused Nigerians.

If the construal of my dreams that there would still be a country called Nigeria to salvage is correct, I am high with the hope of salvaging the very bad situation.

Why should the agents of government even tyrannize me, when they have left an Islamic cleric up north alone to talk free and act freely, depressing our revered army in their fight against the terrorists ravaging our schools and country? He uses the most exotic cars to cruise around and has openly claimed knowledge of all the terrorists and bandits and doing business with them. He has swanked that the government is aware of his escapades with the terrorists and bandits, which he had confessed are Fulani men, and in his words, "only seeking ransoms to survive, but are not criminals". If Baba Bubu and the agents of government have pretended not to have heard him, why should they hear of, and care about me? If the security agents of the country can escort him to the forests to deliver ransoms to Fulani terrorists and bandits, why should they mind a mere writer in his poor room, who has no knife or gun in his hand, but has only made himself available for God's use? I, therefore, plead with all Nigerians to pray that anybody who wishes to fight this grace of God in me would be disgraced.

<u>Grassed</u>

The younger ones of my country have been so oppressed in a country they had called their own. So much so that they have lost hope in the country, because those who have imposed themselves as their leaders have betrayed the little trust the people had managed to have in them. The so called leaders of the country have confused the means with the ends in politics and power. Instead of them to do unto the younger ones what they had wished the past generations of leaders done unto them, they have begun to eat the seed yam sowed by their past generations. Now, the younger generations wish they were never born here.

All that Nigerian youths witness daily in President Baba Bubu's regime are the flows of innocent blood and daily mass burials. They see how the Fulani herdsmen would slaughter innocent farmers in their hundreds, with corpses littering everywhere, after they would have deliberately invaded the farms with their cows to eat up all the crops while the nearby grasses would be begging the cows to munch them, and without any consequence. Yet, Baba Bubu tactically excluded this prime factor responsible for food insecurity and escalated prices of food stuffs in the country, simply because it implicates his Fulani tribe. He heaped the problem on the invisible and unconquerable middlemen. Who are the mysterious middlemen in a country that is said to have a president? Nigerian youths witness how the soldiers are sent to kill innocent civilians who agitate for self-actualizations in the south, particularly in the South-East, because of the President's bigotry approach to governance. This high handed approach is turning those otherwise peaceful youths into terrorists, because "those who made peace negotiation impossible make violence inevitable". They witness how the soldiers themselves are massively set up to be killed by the state backed terrorists in ambushes. They witness how some innocent top ranking soldiers who do not believe in the mere superficial approach to the war against the masquerading criminals are either killed or dismissed. They witness how the terrorists would slaughter human beings as if humans were cows and post the horror videos for public viewing. They witness how school children are kidnapped and killed by bandits in the north, while in all, the presidency would merely express regrets for the loss of lives and Nigerians would helplessly move on to another episode.

Like in a civil war situation, the President would be excited seeing his kinsmen burning down property, children, and the elderly of a whole village of another tribe. This is something that is even categorized as a war crime. These kinds of death are what we used to hear of in the Middle East, which we called "Far", and we wondered how they survived from birth to adulthood. We had thought that such deaths and terrors were far from Nigeria. It only took a man with a bitter heart to make Nigeria one of the endangered countries; where others now wonder how people survive from birth to adulthood in "far" away Nigeria.

As a way of pretending to be doing something about the killings by his Fulani herdsmen, Baba Bubu had to convene a meeting of a certain group in a core northern state, under whose umbrella the killers operate. The meeting was to negotiate with them to stop the killings. The government offered the organization One Hundred Billion Naira, but the organization openly demanded One Hundred and Sixty Billion Naira. Imagine! These and such strategies are only their prior designs to make money out of the rest of us. It is their gain of a faith that can be called Bubuism, which they had invested serious energies and sacrificed lives in its pursuit. They understand that all of them cannot be in the government of Bubuism, provided they can create their own powers and get the patronage of the government. Therefore, they have to help themselves before it is all over; they are so far enjoying the government of Bubuism they fought to enthrone. All they needed so badly and got was the man they could trust to be in the government; for they certainly knew from the onset what they were set to make out of it. This was why they took a break in the killings and maiming during the build up to the second term of their benefactor – Baba Bubu - but gullible Nigerians thought the horror was over.

The governor of the northern state in which the meeting was hosted was shamelessly proud that the President was committed to peace. However, some questions still beg for answers; why has the head of the organization the President met with been moving freely and threatening the nation with more killings without the security operatives doing something? Why did the country need to have another Islamic cleric who boldly admitted being a godfather to the bandits, defending them every day, every time and everywhere? Why is the President looking the other way concerning them but pursuing mere unarmed agitators for self-determinations in the South-West and South-East, and therefore provoking multiplicity of terrorism? And who would ever be able to cure Nigeria of these diseases and bring her citizens together again to love themselves irrespective of regions and religion? That surely is the first liability of Baba Bubu's successor; and as a brief retrospect, are the southern and middle-belt soldiers who fought in the civil war for one Nigeria not disappointed and ashamed of Nigeria of today? Was Col. Odumegu Ojukwu of blessed memory, not a man who saw the future? Well, I guess those soldiers, including my father; Henry Aigbe Igberaese of blessed memory (ever before he gave birth to me) did not, after all, fight for any cause they believed in. They fought for their employment and their survival. Maybe they were ignorant of what would become of the future of their unborn children and generations, including me, the only child left behind in the world by one of the "Federal Soldiers', as we heard that they were called. They were only men who were limited by their time; only if they too had seen the future.

Even the President's supporters are now weary of Nigeria's situation. They can no longer defend the lies of the government. The most they could record as his achievement is that the citizens now know how to take their safety and security seriously or be prudent. That is, Nigerians have learned to be their own soldiers or to adjust to hunger, and to reduce the overall welfare of their households. Self-defense is only for those who have guns or can afford some private guards by cornering the nation's police while those who do not can be slaughtered like fowls. The adjustments are for those who still have some spaces for adjustment while those who no longer have can either continuously increase the suicide rate in the country or be stressed to premature deaths. In all, that there are increasing numbers female headed households, and more people are being added to the core poor; to make poverty endemic and permanent in Nigeria does not in any way bother Baba Bubu. What is most important to him is how his Fulani tribe would forcefully conquer the land they said Allah has given to them. If indeed Allah has given them any land, would Allah send them to war to die before they would possess their inheritance from Him?

Gloominess

The forces in my dreams have continued to torment me for my failure to convey the whole purpose of the dreams to those concerned; putting pen to paper for posterity. The debates between my innermost disputants that "it is safer to write" and "it is safer not to write", the timekeeper and the judge, have now become too much for my small head that I must take a decision fast on which of my inner selves wins. The touches of melancholy have been unbearable since my silence, and more than the fears of mere mortals that I had envisaged; to the extent that I have no option now than to narrate these lamentations; my dreams. So, I have decided to give myself the amity and glee that God has offered me, and the only way I can achieve that peace of mind, set before me by the Almighty God, is to so narrate my dreams. After all, what could I have dreamt of that is new? What are the words that have not been spoken? As my tormentors had asked me for refusing to write, did my early Catholic Church catechist not also tell me that Joseph's brothers only ended up with those thoughts and actions, which show that mere mortals and are greatly limited? If I refuse to write, what would I gain? What would the society gain?

It will be well with my country, Nigeria. And our generations yet unborn would know what we went through in the hands of our fellow black politicians, Baba Bubu and the Fulani herdsmen. They would know how the adherents of Bubuism turned our tormentors in their land conquering quests that led to ethnic hatred, and what led to our kind of *Mau Mau* Movements in the South-East. Then, in our case, what we used our thumbs to bring upon ourselves at the polls in 2015, which we repeated in 2019.

Obliviousness

I have said that I am not annoyed and have declared that I love Nigeria. If in the events that I however become exasperated of the situation in the land that I become so maddened and thus go insensitive in my approach, I still plead with you to pardon my callousness. After all, it was with similar infuriation that every abnormality had become normal that the biblical Apostle Paul dished out his first epistle to the Corinthians in tears and in anger, which later formed a very important book in the Holy Bible. I plead with you to pardon me for five reasons:

1. My descriptions are mere dreams and as is too well known, dreams are intensive in narration and are spontaneous of humans, but inspirational of God to speak to all men concerned with any matter. And who am I not to heed the call of God? Do I even have the strength to plan my words before I write?

2. The Senior Special Assistant to President Baba Bubu on Media and Publicity, other government officials, and Baba Bubu's kinsmen have been insensitive to the status quo in the country, and are consistently against any person who critiques their principal. The Senior Special Assistant has told the governor of Benue State that despite his shrieks for his people who were massively slaughtered by Fulani herdsmen, the killing will continue. He said that the killing would not stop until the governor cooperates with Baba Bubu's government to allow the Fulani herdsmen take over their lands. He has told Rev. Fr. Ejike Mbaka, an ordained Catholic Priest that he is everything except what he claims. By implication, Rev. Fr. Mbaka is not called by God. He has passed unpleasant judgments on Bishop Matthew Hassan Kukah, including that the Catholic Bishop does not behave as a Man of God. These are matters that are supposed to be resolved by God alone. Yet, he is the worst presidential spokesman

to be compared to others across the world because he has never analyzed any policy made by his principal. He says things he does not even believe in. Baba Bubu's Fulani kinsmen have openly threatened that Nigeria would know no peace if the southern governors pass laws against open grazing of cows in their respective states, and nobody has been arrested; nothing has happened.

3. The bandits had stormed the National Army Academy; the very army base, kidnapped soldiers and killed a senior army officer, displaying a horrible video of how they had killed the soldier. Baba Bubu said he did not die in vain, whereas every Nigerian knew that the Baba Bubu meant that he had just died in vain because Fulani bandits had only killed an "Igbo infidel". Otherwise, what else has been done about it since then? And when such bandits are satisfied with killings, they would be asked to feign repentance, get rehabilitated, and get enlisted into the country's army. They need not start from the entry point of recruitment. They could jump-start their careers in the army from the rank of Major since they had already mastered how to shoot better guns than those of the soldiers of the Nigeria Army.

4. Baba Bubu's Ministers have been busy explaining why care must be taken in declaring bandits terrorists. What a sentiment? However, the Indigenous People of Biafra, intensifying the call for self-determination resulting from Baba Bubu's misrule has long ago been declared a terrorist group, without observing any protocol. He later did declare the bandit anyway, partly because his cabal woke up to discover that America was not taking it easy with them and that they were unable to make banditry

spread to the south, no matter how much they had tried. His infamous Minister of Information has provoked Nigerians when he said that the fact that bandits have started collecting taxes from communities in parts of the north does not mean that they have taken over the communities. What of the night invasions of the homes of judges by security operatives; just to intimidate them? In one of such night invasions, a court indicted the Attorney General of the Federation and Minister of Justice as misleading it into issuing a search warrant. Yet, the Attorney General owes nobody any apology, let alone resignation.

5. Since the onset of the Baba Bubu's government, insensitivity and callousness have become extra-constitutional functions of government. These come in the forms of lop-sided appointments, distributions of wealth, and in speeches in favour of his Fulani clan. Nothing can be more insensitive than to have a president who is a national disaster. Nothing can be more insensitive than the President's passionate hatred for the South-Eastern region of the country, and but for the oil that the country can never do without, my South-South region.

I can continue to mention the deliberate provocations and even assaults the Baba Bubu's government has meted on Nigerians, but that would make this book excessively voluminous.

Patriotism

However, we are still lucky to have fearless patriots like Gov. Nyesom Wike, Sen. Enyinnaya Abaribe and Mazi Nnamdi Kanu, the Leader of the Indigenous People of

Biafra (IPOB), amongst many others, who have continued to tackle him.

This Mazi Nnamdi Kanu
In whom the unity of Nigeria finds more expressions.
His incarceration will free Nigeria
His suffering will heal the wounds of Nigerians
There is a reason for this.

We have the Christian clerics, Bishop Matthew Hassan Kukah, and Bishop David Oyedepo and the literary icon Prof. Wole Soyinka to thank. Oh! Bishop David Oyedepo, because of whose voice against nepotism, injustice, and oppression, the government of Baba Bubu got angry and attempted to use the Corporate Affairs Commission to emasculate, enervate and debilitate the Christian Churches. If a clergyman would not rise against injustice and oppression, what else would he have to do to justify his calling? Concerning David Oyedepo, a man who has employed Nigerians more than any State Government in the federation except perhaps, Lagos State, a country that knows what it is doing would have long decorated him with the highest National Honour an individual can get.

Just look at how the Attorney General of the Federation and Minister of Justice, who has assumed supremacy in a country of injustice, celebrated the arrest of Nnamdi Kanu with a world press conference, as if he had won a Noble Prize. He did so with all his might and soul, as if that was the reason he was appointed. He first spoke on such national issue in his Hausa-Fulani language, to deceive poor northerners that it was in their best interests he acted. And that he, their champion, has subdued their common enemy, whereas terrorists and bandits have continued to brutalize them. This was at a time terrorists had ceased Local Governments Areas and electing parallel governors and hosting their flags in parts of the north. Yet, he did not raise any alarm and suggest any state of emergency rule as he did on the killings in the South-East. What a shame! In short, no matter how bad insecurity situation is in the south, it can never be compared to that confronting his northern brothers. No matter the level and incidence of poverty in the south, it can never be compared to that in the north. Yet, these are never sufficient for the Minister to strategize and raise a national alarm in Hausa-Fulani language.

By the way, is it not surprising that the government of Nigeria has such intelligence to arrest Kanu and Igboho, with the same government pretending not to know how to arrest the bandits and kidnappers? Yes, only because of where they come from; a lawless government, merely wishing its citizens to obey its laws.

I earnestly hope that indeed, there would still be Nigeria – it would eventually be impossible without the restructuring Baba Bubu hates with a passion. Baba Bubu must learn from history. He should know that when Louis XIV decided to persecute the Huguenots, it harmed France so greatly because the Huguenots were one of the most hard working groups of France. The expulsion of the Huguenots was actually what severely hurt France's economy. He should know that the South-East has the highest Gross Domestic Products in the whole of West Africa.

Sectionalism

I feel it was highly commendable when the Federal Government under the regime of Olusegun Obasanjo introduced the Universal Basic Education, under which the basic level of education has been made free and compulsory for every child in Nigeria. The school feeding programme was also a good initiative but Baba Bubu has now made it too sectional to be reckoned with. He has been a president for a section of the country – not even the whole of the north, and he has no clue of what is going on with the programme.   The Goodluck Jonathan's regime focus on basic education could also be said to be too sectional and completely a misplacement of priorities and waste of resources. He focused mostly on the integration of the almajiri in the northern part of the country, as if he could force a horse to drink water from the river he had forced it to. He did not expect the benefiting region to appreciate him for destroying their age long almajiri culture. Nevertheless, he meant well for them and only God on His heavenly throne would judge the northern elites if the children of Baba Bubu, and all the governors in the region are among these almajiri children who are to sustain their culture of destitution. Perhaps, President Goodluck Jonathan did not understand that for any plan to succeed, the targets of the plan must first be enthusiastic about it, and in need of the programmes of such a plan. At least, with his establishment of universities to make every state has at least, one Federal University, President Goodluck Jonathan did something substantial about higher education, which has remained an unbeaten legacy.

This polarization of the country along sectional lines was/is part of the obnoxious policies that are setting the country backward. Policies that are designed to favour the weak at the expense of the strong are not incentives for the weak to be strong but enticements for them to be weaker. They are also made disincentives for the strong to be stronger. The much talked about Value–Added-Tax is a typical example. Instead of finding a way to appeal to the strong, to voluntarily carry the weak along in the spirit of "Let's Be Our Brother's Keeper", they want brothers to keep brothers by force, and to use Plato's words, "much against their will".

As an academic, I have seen my northern friends presenting papers in national and international conferences and getting proud of their regional deficiencies and widespread poverty. That is all because they would advocate/recommend more courtesies from the national treasury for the northern region. Once they introduce their papers, it becomes very easy to know where they are heading – no suspense at all; mostly predetermined researches. In short, they are usually mere essays of widespread poverty and insecurity in the north.

During the recent coronavirus pandemic, a northern friend argued with me that if the Federal Government had any palliatives to give to Nigerians, it would be better to face the northern poor since they were more susceptible and vulnerable. This was against the facts that it was in Lagos and Ogun states, with Abuja, the same Federal Government had declared a total lockdown. His argument was very witty; that what the indigenes of Lagos State could produce and save in a month was equal to what those poor indigenes of Kano State could save in six months. In other words, given that he used Lagos and Kano to represent the south and the north respectively, one southern is equal to six northerners in terms of productivity and savings. What a retrogressive way of thinking! I simply gave up the argument and he probably thought that he had won. Indeed, he thanked me for my patience in listening to him.

Therefore, instead of working to diminish Gunnar Myrdal's "backwash effect", and striving to propagate his "spread effect", where developments in the fast developing regions would positively affect the lesser developing regions, it has become the case of an inverted "backwash effect", where the underdevelopments in the lesser developed regions adversely affect the fast developing regions. This leads to the backwardness of the entire country because in keeping with an African proverb, whenever the lame person imposes himself in front of his fast walking partner, both of them must inevitably stop walking. When they hear these things, they tell the northern youths that the words amount to anti-north sentiments, even as they would brainwash them against reading this book. So, how may God help us, as stated in the last line in the joke that is referred to as the country's national pledge?

However, have we not had northerners of Fulani extraction such as Shehu Usman Aliyu Shagari and Umaru Musa Yar'dua, both of blessed memory, as Presidents of this country? Yes, we have had! They held the country together. They did not need to do appointments and allocate resources in lopsided manner or give any tacit approval for the dogs, the monkeys and the baboons to be soaked in blood by their Fulani tribesmen, to deserve being loved by the north or their Fulani tribesmen. They did not practice religious and tribal chauvinism and bigotry while in government. They did not, using their body languages, encourage ethnic jingoism and narrow mindedness in governance. Nobody cared whether they were northerners or not! And so, there was no hues and cry in their time the way it is all over the land today. As far as Baba Bubu and his praise-singers are concerned, Shehu Shagari and Yar'dua were neither true Fulani nor true Muslims.

When Yar'dua was seriously ill, countrymen and women were not forced to fast and pray for him in Churches and Mosques; they voluntarily did. When it pleased the Almighty God that it happened, and drawing from an Esan adage, it simply turned out to be the case that the sweet soup was not enough to eat the pounded yam, everybody became exceedingly sorrowful with his death. Yes, sorrowful, despite some misgivings surrounding the management of his illness and the crookedness of a cabal who wanted to take advantage of his illness. I guess he died only because the citizens could not stop the coward called death. This contrasts sharply with the strong negative sentiments that the vast majority of Nigerians, including some members of his cabinet and his supposed aficionado governors when Baba Babu in 2018, took ill. In the end, it turned out to be a complete reversal of the Esan adage in which the bad soup became too much to eat the pounded yam; only a few among those who cooked it would continue to eat, joyfully and thankfully!

Why would it take government campaigns and threats to force citizens to stop praying openly and wishing their beloved president dead? As a citizen, I wish to reserve my thoughts concerning the diffident oxymoron about the ill health and education of my president, Baba Bubu (or any other one for that matter). I do have the right to do so; more so that to cover up his shame in governance, he has attempted to justify his narrow mindedness by telling the country that tribalism and sectionalism are not the problems we have in our country. In other words, it does not matter that he continues to be a bigot. That he is not even ready to repent because he does not see anything wrong in encouraging his kinsmen into committing crimes against the country and protecting them to wreak havoc on others as a problem from which he ought to desist. That is the much a country gets when the buck stops at the table of a person with doubtful educational credentials!

Chapter Two

General Introduction Continued

Humanism

If I ever become a governor, I would focus more attention on the human capital development; the elements of health and education than playing to the gallery with everything. This would develop the potentials in our youths for higher national outputs. This is because human beings matter most. Yes, many may not see my achievements in office as a governor, but the quality human beings would. Teachers, especially those in the rural areas, need smithereens of training and good remunerations for the profession to be prestigious and attractive to brains.

There has to be a way of recognizing the real indigent students who need attention to proceed after their compulsory basic education. There has to be the establishment of the state counterpart of Education Trust Fund to fund research proposals and developments in the state tertiary institutions where majority of our youths are found; for our main problem is that our development policies are not based on research outcomes. There has to be a radical departure from the current intergenerational transmission of poverty, especially for many small families and female headed families. That is, a deliberate transfer of income from the rich segments to the poor segments of the society. There has to be policies to encourage production and discourage wasteful consumption. There has to be a farewell to the Out-of-Pocket model of healthcare delivery towards the combinations of all fantastic models, and with researchers developing indigenous ones that can fit into our system or replace the orthodox models.

As a matter of fact, co-insurance and innovations for the rural communities and the informal sector are urgently needed. Thus, there is need for the creation of a pre-existing "sickness fund" and education fund, so that the process of delivery healthcare and education services would meet the basic four dimensions; availability, accessibility, utilization, and stability. No child, who could become the best president of this country should die from infant epidemiological concerns, or not realize near his full educational potentials. No elderly person should die from avoidable age related diseases, making aging a dreadful syndrome. No woman should die from maternal complications in the process of bringing another person to life (this earth), simply because she is poor.

Baba Bubu, upon his return from a fifteen month medical trip in the United Kingdom in 2018, for which his life now depends on how long the United Kingdom and their doctors wish, had told the citizens with pride, how technology had rescued him from the jaw of death. It was expected that at least, before the end of his tenure, he would replicate even a little bit of such machines that are capable of challenging and defeating death in a country he had sworn to protect. Unfortunately, history will never be kind to him as a man who "out of his own obscurity discovers his mission" and betrayed it. Yet, all his frequent medical check-up had been in the United Kingdom, except during the period of COVID-19 pandemic in 2020 when United Kingdom doctors were allegedly brought into the presidential palace to artificially keep him buoyant. All these have been done in the country at undisclosed costs – grand corruption.

Contrary to his campaign promises, he has not only failed to ban medical tourism, he has in fact become the president who has been engaged the most in medical tourism in the history of all nations, at least as far back as human memory can recollect, all of which have been at a colossal expense of the public purse. Since he has been involved, abnormal medical tourisms have become normal among the politicians and the elites, leading to huge foreign exchange outflow from the country in the face of recklessly abandoned of the health sector in Nigeria. Then, the most articulate lawmaker in the House of Representatives, from Esan North East/Esan South East Federal Constituency, Hon. Sergius Ogun nearly became an enemy to all his allies in both the Upper and Lower Chambers for dare to sponsor a bill against medical tourism and education tourism by the children of the political elites, elected or appointed. Unfortunately, the most progressive bill that was ever tabled in the House for discussion was killed by corruption, as the sponsor was hushed down by the vast majority of his colleagues in the supposedly hallowed chamber while they demanded of him the outright withdrawal of the bill. Fortunately and to the admiration of his supporters, the

Honourable gentleman stubbornly refused to withdraw the bill in a determined effort to be on the right side of history.

<u>Personality</u>

I had raised issues about an ideal governor in Nigeria because the governor would matter most in the Nigeria of my dreams. Such a governor should not be the typical politician whose only ambition is to develop strategies to take his larceny to the next level and outdo his predecessors in office. He should not be a person who is interested in the unhealthy competition of highest looting. He must be intelligent enough – not the self-acclaimed technocrats all around, but those with sound empirical proofs of having been technocrats overtime. He should be a governor who can attract global grants to the critical sectors of health and education, not a person whose only source of independent income is borrowing out the lives of future generations. He should be one whose aggregate makeup has risen to the level that has astonished global grant agencies, such that they would be attracted to, and trust him enough to naturally follow him into the affairs of the state with their capitals on their backs. This is because our resources will never be enough, even if we have to tax all our primary school pupils. I am convinced that such men (women), who could make the so called state's share from the federation account a child's play, and then, downplay the loathsome and repugnant crowding out taxation are not attractive to the office. They are only afraid of the murky waters of politics and as such, they have become armchair critics and onlookers while the illiterates become the philosophers in the country.

The reason for their fears is evident; before the 1999 return to civil rule in the country, not many people believed that the military would hand over power to the civilians, because of their past failures of similar stories of prospects; to honour their promise to quit the political scene and withdraw to the barracks where they rightly belong! Therefore, it was mostly the charlatans, hooligans, swindlers and at best, the retirees, who had nothing to lose should the military not honour their words once again, that participated in the process and got hold of power from the beginning. They had followed the pattern of their military predecessors in power to loot the country dry in their attempts to drain out the blood of the future generations. They have since held the country to ransom. Now, those who are incapable of being led have become the leaders. Those who are incapable of being taught have become the teachers. Those who are incapable of thinking have become the philosophers, mistaking their injudicious ideas as policies. They can now sit down in their covens to plan and fund coups against the people. They do not want to see professionals around them. They hate technocrats or any intelligent and sincere person. They do not want any disequilibrium in the way they have fraudulently learned to corner the collective resources of the country. They have constituted themselves into a clique that has laid hold to the country's wealth. Yet, the people pretend not to understand why the system is fast collapsing, even more than they can see. Now that a dislocation of the status quo is setting in, they cannot be happy that the old order is gradually being defeated. They will resist the new order.

Of course, Baba Bubu does not know that patriotism is only a reciprocal curve of a leader's commitments to the wellbeing of his country's citizens. He believes that the youths are nothing but a bunch of lazy and good for nothing seekers of government jobs. He is, therefore, quick to remind them that there are no government jobs for them, even when it is that he has lived off the government all the days of his life! They had only told him what John Fitzgerald Kennedy (May 29, 1917 – November 22, 1963), had told American youths; to think of what they can do for America, and not what America can do for them. Unfortunately, they did not explain the context in which Kennedy had made that statement; that the many kinds of stuff America had already done for American youths were not at all in contention. The American youth was already guaranteed food. The American youth was already guaranteed clothes. The American youth was already guaranteed a home. The American youth was already guaranteed healthcare. The American youth was already guaranteed education, social security, security of life and property, befitting job with more than a living wage. In the unlikelihood of dying (young), the American youth was guaranteed a decent burial. In the unlikely event that such death was unnatural, the American youth was guaranteed of revenge, so that he would not be among the souls crying daily to God to avenge his deaths; his God's given president would have already done that. May I now ask; what the Nigerian youth, who is not the Yusufu Baba Bubu, is guaranteed?

Structuralism

I did not add that such a governor should not be interested in a second tenure. I would rather say there should be no second tenure for governors and the President to be enshrined in the new Constitution, in order to stabilize the political system. Here again, they will be fast to point to American democracy, as if, as Adebayo has put it, the new orthodoxy needs end in "Reaganomics and Thatcherism". Most of the hostilities in many states of the federation, detracting even angels as governors from good performance are about second tenures. A governor could successfully attract numerous development partners through Memoranda of Understanding, but no "flying geese" would land with its capital amid fights, battles, troubled and unstable system. Any investor is likely to be a "bear" than a "bull".

President Goodluck Jonathan was close to entrenching this structural legacy, but it was a little too small and a little too late, with perhaps the fear of the northern cabals, which held him back in giving life to the constitutional conference he had convoked. He got both the needed "popular enthusiasm and public cooperation" as "the petrol and lubricating oil for the engine of development" for such decisions that would have set the country free and on a new path of progress. At least, a six year straight single tenure would have been entrenched. The corrections of the other constitutional anomalies and observed empirical irregularities would have been finalized in that conference. They would, only if he had applied that which brought him to office as the President; the "Doctrine of Necessity", as a smart way of overcoming any human obstacle against the progress of the country. Indeed, he had the singular opportunity of demonstrating a six-year tenure as president, not too short to stamp his feet and fix all that are wrong with our constitution, without considering a second tenure. A six-year tenure is not too short as a gestation period for policies to fully manifest from their conceptions, but

President Goodluck Jonathan blew it by stretching his luck too far and desired to be a champion of two worlds. This is what I consider as his only slipup in government, which gave birth to the messy and chaotic leadership we have in the country today.

He played along with the northern and Fulani elements in that conference. They believed that the north was not ready for "restructuring" the conference tended towards; for they fear that word like perdition. If you think this is a lie, just mention "restructure" to any of them and they will instantly hate you. This is because, to them, there is no difference between "restructure" and "division", and they had taught their children so. Let me ask; what is it of all the ways that would make the country great that the northern oligarchy have ever been ready for? They were not ready for independence in 1954. They are not ready for resource control. They are not ready for appointment by merit in the civil service and political offices. They are not ready to review the constitution and move with the dynamics of time. They are not ready to develop their resources and collect their taxes. They are not ready for the right education for their children. They are not ready for admission by merit, even into the unity schools, let alone the universities. They are not ready for Igbo presidency, and they are not even ready to read this book.

What this means is that the rest of the country; the Middle-Belt and the entire south should continue to wait till the north is ready. Ask the very vocal leaders among them of their views on true federalism; they would never be straightforward with their answers to the simple question. They would play to the gallery; to be applauded by their southern collaborators who have the same personal interests that have beclouded their senses of reasoning. And thus, many of them are always afraid to say something that would annoy the northern cabal. Instead of an answer to the simple question, they would dance around corruption, which though a leadership problem, they think is an economic policy. Yet, Nigerian leaders and the party in power fear the word "Revolution"; something that will come like a thief in the night, sometime, someday, to wipe them all out, whether they keep arresting and persecuting, the "Revolution Now" theorist(s) or not. They do not even know he is a mere "John the Baptist", not qualified for the coming revolution. Little wonder that the popular Senator, Enyinnaya Abaribe had to tell them that those who live by propaganda will die by propaganda – a mere derivation from a portion of the Holy Bible; for those who live by the sword shall die by the sword.

If anybody would contend that a six year single term for the President and the governors is too short to make impacts in government (let he even increase it to seven), then, eight years of the present two terms would not still be enough. The example of the headship of the country's universities is good enough in this regard. In those bad old days, when the Vice Chancellors needed second tenures of four years after their first of four years, cultism, gangsters, hooliganism used to be rife among the students who were being used against opposing interests, and instabilities were predominant in the systems. These vices rationally and greatly reduced the moment it became a single term of five years, because the Vice Chancellors did not have need for the cultists; to fight perceived enemies and up their games. They began to think of how to write their names in gold; a kind of healthy competition to surpass their predecessors in office. Therefore, we approached a kind of the Robert Solow's Model of the "Golden Rule of Accumulations". The Vice Chancellors began to be more focused on how to do unto their future generations what they had wished their past generations done unto them.

Assurances

For the umpteenth time, I have no human witness that this book is specifically ordained of me to write. Not even my wife, with whom I regularly share my bed, and many times, completely cloak myself in her, while the wider part of our bed cries to be occupied, can testify to my dreams. She cannot because no matter what we do together in our bed, our nervous systems can never work together. Should anybody still decide to dispute that I did dream, or contend that I am inspired by the Almighty God, let them believe what they want to believe. All I can say is that this book is only part of the many pains in me about our country. It is my genuine desire to let our succeeding generations know some of the sorrows that we, who would become their past generations, had gone through in the hands of those who we used our thumbs, at the polling booth, to bring to power. Once again, I have no other option than to follow Apostle Paul to say we have no other custom. Then, let that person pardon 'my poor attitude', as I am, after all, not a genius and a mastermind.

If however a declaration is the only way to convince all and sundry that even the source of the title of this book is a dream, you can all see that I did not mind; I have already taken it.

CHAPTER THREE

Once Great

Nigeria! A country once acclaimed to be great, is supposed to be a giant economy in Africa. Nigeria! A country, which was at a point, one of the twenty fastest growing economies in the world, has never had it so bad. Nigerians have elected a president who is intelligence dead, except on the matters of nepotism. They have elected a president who never acted as the country's president but only serves the narrow interests of his very tiny ethnic group, whose only wish is to dominate the vast majority of the people by force. The President they have elected among millions of intellectuals is an incapacitated man that serves some tiny interests whose definition of politics is the subornation of general interests to those of individual interests. So, Nigerians elected a president at whose table the buck appears not to stop, but at the table of the cabal he has created to run the affairs of the country. They not only speak for him, they do virtually everything for him without him knowing what they said that he had said. It is highly doubtful whether the President, who was been termed a man of integrity, and the best Nigerian president that never was; if he were not elected, knows what Twitter is or not. When journalists once asked him questions on what his handlers had said he had tweeted, he thought that they were insulting him.

"You journalists in this country are not patriotic at all. Nigeria is the only country in the world where citizens would say their president twitter (sic)", he said, with all the seriousness it deserves when a president of a country is being insulted. Unfortunately, some foreign journalists were in their midst.

What did his handlers do? They simply destroyed the legacy "Presidential Media Chat" (PMC) of the past presidents, instituted by a man who is so far arguably the best president of Nigeria in this republic, President Olusegun Obasanjo, herein referred to as Baba Obasara for the love I have for him. Ironically, Baba Obasara was the same person who later cracked the kernel that the fowl has swallowed. That is, he was key among those who brought the punishment and monumental disaster, Baba Bubu upon this country.

The PMC was a popular programme in which the people who elected the President had opportunities to sit with him on live radio and television programmes. With it, the people heard from their elected president directly instead of only hearing from his spokesmen who often use their discretions on matters of critical and urgent public importance. The past presidents had used it to capture the minds of Nigerians and had given them the needed sense of belonging. The programme had doused tensions on critical and sensitive issues in the country, so much so that the people began to trust their governments once again. It gave the people the confidence that at least, their presidents knew what was happening, even though they were yet to be in charge.

So, when Baba Bubu, came on board as the new president, he too wanted to win that confidence of the people using the PMC. Unfortunately, the very first one was a complete disaster. Indeed, it brought shame upon his handlers and admirers. Diaspora Nigerians began to lament. Foreign journalists, who had drawn the people's attention to the emptiness of Baba Bubu during the campaign in which he was always shielded off the crowd, began to reinforce their documentaries. The documentaries had wondered why out of millions of intellectuals Nigeria is blessed with, such an empty brained fellow, who could not even pronounce the names of his party and running mate, was the person the people could find to be their president. Since that disastrous PMC, Nigerians have never heard any original word from their president again. It has only been words from the "Presidency", instead of the "President"; and whatever the Presidency says is now what the President has said. Worse still is that it is a presidency in which everybody speaks without coordination, provided he is a member of the ruling cabal, now led by the Minister of Justice and Attorney General of the Federation.

The cabal was formerly led by the late Chief of Staff. It has some people who are only pretending to be members simply because they are also in the President's cabinet. They are in the cabinet only at the mercy of each member of the cabal, to whom each member of the cabinet or anybody holding any relevant political office must report if he is to remain in government, not in power. It is unbelievable that many senators and members of the House of Representatives, who though were elected, have since seen themselves as appointees of the cabal, especially when in search of contracts or money to share among themselves. As representatives of the people, they hardly have time to sit down to discuss progress. Ironically too, many governors barely stay in their states but run around the presidency and the cabal for what only God knows.

Imagine one man, in the bid to remain in an office, commits his time and money to appease each member of the cabal, so that whenever his matter is being tabled, they would all speak in his favour. Then, when the cabinet is being reconstituted, his name would reappear, at least, to deceive his people that he too, is part of the show going on in Abuja, the city capital of Nigeria. This raises the question of how much time such a person would have to do his job as a Minister or to perform in whatever capacity he finds himself. Why would he not be as poor as a church rat within a year of leaving office, despite the stealing and looting? Has he not only been stealing for his superiors – members of the cabal? These members include even those who hold no official positions but are just hanging around the presidential office and are well known to be among those remotely controlling the old and frail man Nigerians elected as their president.

Imagine elected senators, forsaking their beautiful red chamber, just to go round each member of the cabal, if they must be returned for an everlasting term. These include some opposition senators establishing loyalties to the cabal, if the Economic Crime Commission's dogs would not be let loose on them. How much time would they have to think and consult with their constituents, let alone time to compose a quality bill, especially those who are so afraid of their shadows that they can only employ intellectually deficient persons like then as legislative aids?

Once upon a time, there were two people; Adam Aliyu Oshiomhole, also called Eric, herein referred to as Oshemore for the love I have for him, and Ibrahim Magu, herein referred to as Ibra Maga for the love I have for him, who had belatedly tried to be independent in their jobs as Chairman of the ruling party and head of the Crime watchdog respectively. The duo tried to build stronger institutions rather than building strong individuals. They thought that they were doing the right thing by administering mere Panadol tablets to cure cancer. They were easily booted out by the cabal, because they were merely in government but mistakenly thought that they were in power. The detail of this episode is outside the scope of this book.

Chapter Four

Political Bourgeoisie

The Nigerian political bourgeoisie, who see themselves as the capitalists and feudal lords of the country while the electorates are their proletariats and the serfs, have not realized that they are poorer than their counterparts elsewhere. This is despite their being among the highest remunerated in the world and with the loopholes in the Nigerian constitution and system that enable stealing. They are yet to realize that even the teachers in the country, who they daily deny the fruits of their labour, are richer than them. Let me explain:

Firstly, they are the most financially unstable set of people. At that point when they began to steal the money; the amount they have never seen before, they raise their consumption levels, even in violation of the Keynesian psychological law of consumption. The Keynesian postulation is explained in the simple Keynesian Consumption Function:

$$C = a + bY \qquad (1)$$

Where: C = consumption; a = the intercept; the part of consumption that is independent of income, b = the slope; the level of consumption that depends on income and Y = Income

John Maynard Keynes (1883 -1946) had explained that men and women tend to raise their consumption level as their incomes increase, but not as much as the increase in incomes. However in Nigeria, the slope, which is the rate of the rise in consumption as income is increasing, becomes even higher during that phase in which they experience rise in income than Keynes had envisaged.

They plan as if they own this world, expecting other citizens to fold their hands, watch and wait for them to keep increasing their income (more often than not, ill-gotten) unchallenged. They easily forget that the world is about competition; that the fact that they started well does not necessarily mean that they would end well. The moment when the opportunity is all over, comes sooner than they expected, but with the slope refusing to fall even as income falls.

J. M. Keynes

John Maynard Keynes was an English economist, journalist, and financier, recognized in history as an economic theorist. He discussed the causes of protracted unemployment that characterized the era of the Great Depression, as well as other fundamental ideas that transformed the economic policies of governments. His father, John Neville Keynes, also an economist and academic administrator at King's College in Cambridge, first named him Baron. His mother was also a graduate of Cambridge. John Maynard Keynes studied Mathematics at King's College, Cambridge between 1902 and 1905, where he was elected a fellow in 1909. He worked as an economic analyst in the India Office in Whitehall, a teacher at Cambridge, the "de facto" unpaid Financial Manager of British World War I. He was also Britain's Chief Economic Representative to the United States and international fora during and immediately after World War II. His works include: *"Indian Currency and Finance"* (1913), *"The Economic Consequences of the Peace"* (1919), *"Treatise on Probability"* (1921), *"A Tract on Monetary Reform"* (1923), *"A Treatise on Money"* (1930), and many scholarly and journalistic articles. But his most influential work was *"The General Theory of Employment, Interest and Money"* (1935 – 36).

According to the editors of the Encyclopedia Britannica, *"at Cambridge, he was influenced by economist Alfred Marshall, who prompted Keynes to shift his academic interests from mathematics and the classics to politics and economics. Cambridge also introduced Keynes to an important group of writers and artists. The early history of the Bloomsbury group —an exclusive circle of the cultural elect, which counted among its members, Leonard and Virginia Woolf, the painter Duncan Grant, and the art critic Clive Bell — centered upon Cambridge and the remarkable figure of Lytton Strachey. Strachey, who had entered Cambridge two years before Keynes, inducted the younger man into the exclusive private club known simply as "the Society." Its members and associates (some of them homosexual, like Keynes himself) were the leading spirits of Bloomsbury. Throughout his life, Keynes was to cherish the affection and respond to the influence of this group.*

The basic and revolutionary idea of Keynesian economics – that recessions can be mitigated and unemployment more effectively reduced by government spending designed to increase aggregate demand – strongly influenced the fiscal policies of western governments until the 1970s and later inspired successful responses by many governments to the Great Recession of 2007–09".

Nigeria politicians have now shown that Keynes was only an economist of his own England and western environments where the consumer axiom of rationality holds. And that he did not realize that there would be a country of, according to the great Professor of economics in the University of Benin, Hassan Oaikhenan, with "so many paradoxes". He did not realize that there would be a country where men and women can consume higher than the increase in their incomes. So that his psychological law would have added: "…. or more than the increase in income – the coefficient "b" can increase more than the increase in the variable Y, in equation (1). As an economist, I would want to be known for adding this with the following example:

As Nigerian politicians are elected or appointed, in anticipation of the money they would get, they become customers to all the banks in the country, borrowing ahead of income that is not yet earned and engaging in unmaintainable and unsustainable lifestyles – many live on mere promissory notes. They begin to bury a substantial part of the treasures, as we shall see shortly; by Thomas Aquinas. The bank, which has become one of the biggest sources of leakages in the country's economy, begins to help them transfer looted monies in different currencies abroad and importing even woods and saw dust in the name of foreign building materials and furniture. These banks would later put pressure on them, in desperations to recover the money they had given them as consumer loans before they would crash land. Keynes also revealed how this leakage can be with a four sector model of the aggregate economy of a country:

$$Y = C+I+G+(X-M) \qquad (2)$$

Where: Y = National Income or National Outputs; C = Consumption, the highest component of the aggregate economy and usually carried out by the household in the simple circular flow of income. I = Investment, the most important component of the aggregate economy and the primary function of the firms in the simple circular flow of income. G = Government Expenditure, which is autonomous and the primary function of government in the complex circular flow of income. And $(X-M)$ = Net Export, the difference between exports (injection) and imports (leakage) in the complex circular flow of income; making the equation an open economy equation.

$$\text{However, } C = Co + C_1y - C_2r \qquad (3)$$
$$I = Io + I_1y - I_2r \qquad (4)$$
$$G = Go \text{ (for simplicity)} \qquad (5)$$
$$X = Xo \qquad (6)$$
$$M = Mo + M_1y - M_2r \qquad (7)$$

Where: o_s denote autonomous of the variables to which they are attached; y_i are the incomes which the variables (consumption, investment and imports respectively), to which they are attached are dependent on, The r_i are the interest rate, which the variables (consumptions, investments and imports respectively), to which they are attached are dependent on. Incomes have positive relationships with the variables, meaning movements in the same directions; and interest rates have negative relationships with the variables, meaning movements in different directions.

If we substitute equations (3) to (7) into equation (2), we would see that the economy is affected through the multiplier, the derivation of which is beyond the scope of my dreams. However, our interest here is the net export (X - M). With the help of the bankers, politicians transfer the country's investable funds in the form of foreign exchange abroad – which countries who know what they are doing would never willingly do. They increase the import of items that are abundantly produced in the country, thereby constituting leakages in the economy, as imports become larger and larger while foreign exchange becomes smaller and smaller.

Jean-Baptiste Colbert

We may zoom a little into the inspirational life of Jean-Baptiste Colbert (1619 -1683), Lord of Vandières and Cernay, in case it would mean anything to Baba Bubu and his cohort. Colbert was also Secretary of State for the Navy between1668 and 1683 under Louis XIV. In his life career, he almost held great offices of state, like Baba Bubu, though less. He was responsible for developing trade, industry, and the merchant navy. He modernized Paris and sponsored new improvements in the sciences. He presided over the economic policy of France from 1661 till he died in 1683. To Colbert, the expansion of commerce to enhance a favourable balance of trade was the fundamental of state wealth. As a mercantilist, Colbert believed in encouraging flows in the form of bullions into the reserves of the state. He prohibited the export of gold and silver. He subsidized exports and restricted imports. He forbade wealth from leaving France and strived to make the country to be self-sufficient.

"Colbert's central principle was that the wealth and the economy of France should serve the state. Drawing on the ideas of mercantilism, he believed state intervention was needed to secure the largest part of limited resources. To accumulate gold, a country always had to sell more goods abroad than it bought. Colbert also helped establish the Academy of Inscriptions and Medals (1663), the Academy of Sciences (1666), and the Academy of Music (1669). As superintendent for public buildings, he oversaw significant additions to the Louvre as well as the expansion of the palace complex at Versailles", a city where he died peacefully of illness on *6th September 1683.*

In all these, Colbert did something wrong that can never be forgotten and forgiven of him at the detriments of all his contributions to the growth of the French economy; causing and supporting wars.

His major failure *"stemmed from his determination to end Dutch domination of Far Eastern and European trade. Unable to damage the Dutch by a vindictive tariff war, he supported Louis XIV's unprovoked invasion of Holland in 1672 in the hope that the Dutch would be overrun in a few weeks".*

Is that not what the Baba Bubu and his Fulani fellows think of the Igbos and the rest of us? If Colbert who occupied lesser offices than Baba Bubu but did more can so easily be forgotten because of his bitterness and ethnic hatred, who would even write Baba Bubu's history? Of whose interest would it serve except that he has made Nigeria a hell fire? If we do not collectively rise up without fear to either reclaim or rescue our country, hell fire will be better than Nigeria in the future.

Our politicians would never pick up any of the books containing such biographies and any holy books to learn from. They would rather have as their bible, a book like Robert Greene's "The 48 Laws of Power", which they have no stamina to read completely and understand anyway. They simply peruse it and have their minds made up of what they believe Greene must be talking about. They are often wrong because the author wrote some "observations", "keys" and "reversals" in each chapter. Even at that, they do not know that the book is unpolished, unfinished and not a lacquer in spirit, as Greene himself admitted. It is also unprincipled, unethical, dishonourable and unscrupulous, as warned by Greene himself:

...Amoral, cunning, ruthless and instructive... As attention-grabbing in its design as it is in content, the bold volume outlines the laws of power in their unvarnished essence, synthesizing the philosophies of Machiavelli, Santzu, Carl von Clausewitz and other great thinkers. Some laws require prudence ..., some stealth ..., and some total absence of mercy ... " (Robert Greene, Back Cover).

So, it is not the author's fault that they often feed their hearts with garbage and baloney and sow the seeds of their own destructions because they have no strengths to get the end of each chapter, and to read from the front cover to the back cover of the book. They peruse such books to their dooms.

Chapter Five

So Daft

Being so daft, the politicians would normally not understand that the friendship the bankers suddenly developed with them is what Ola Rotimi of blessed memory called "the friendship between the he-goat and the cocoyam". I have seen a banker who needed to catch "this *mugu*" quickly before he leaves office, and that could be at all costs and by any means, including prostitution, if she was a female banker. The banker would never teach his new "friends" how to invest and contribute to the most important component of the aggregate economy, because they have been trained to tell their victims only what their ears inch for.

The result to the politicians is second degree level of poverty, initially unnoticeable to the poor of the mere first degree level; for it is better to learn how to live moderate life style from the beginning than to be flamboyant early and become poor later in life. Whereas property is supposed to appreciate in value, they would begin to sell out what they had acquired with their ill-gotten wealth at prices cheaper than what they had bought them long before; just to survive when incomes finally fall. That is because they had nothing in their noggins when incomes were rising, and then, end up at involuntary zero net savings at their times of death. This is the hypothesis of buried treasures in estates. The alternative hypothesis is unburied treasures in the estate, when the right to acquire property belongs to the individual but the right to use it does not belong to him alone but also to his friends, relatives and the poor. In fear of uncertainty after office, they would want to die in the offices they had held even when the electorates no long want them. They always think the world is their inheritance.

St. Thomas Aquinas

St. Thomas Aquinas (1225 – 1274 A.D.) had propounded such two property rights in the medieval periods (476 A.D. to the 15th century). The implication is acquiring to redistribute.

I believe that this two property rights of Aquinas would make the poor love the rich, and settle the existing conflict between the rich and the poor in the "exciting times". That is, the poor would no longer believe that the rich are the reasons for their problems because the rich would have shown that they no longer believe that the poor are the architects of their misfortunes. The reverse beliefs have cause these "exciting times".

I love St. Thomas Aquinas and what later became the school of thought called Thomism, in which the excellent property rights were originated. I love to talk about him and this school of thought, as our young people would learn from such robust history.

Thomas Aquinas was an Italian Dominican Father and a philosopher, a priest of the Catholic Church, and doctor of the Church. He was hugely a dominant philosopher, theologian, and jurist in the tradition of scholasticism. Aquinas was well known within the jurist tradition as the "Doctor Angelicus, the Doctor Communis, and the Doctor Universalis". He had an interesting childhood occasioned by his parents, who took him to be a prospective monk at the "Benedictine Monastery" at Monte Cassino at age five. At age fourteen, he moved to the University of Naples where he was acquainted with the "Dominican order" and joined the order six years later; at age twenty. He proved to be the greatest of the scholastic philosophers, producing a wide ranging synthesis of Christian theology and Aristotelian philosophy. Thus, he influenced the Catholic doctrine for hundreds of years, and his synthesis was later adopted to be the official philosophy of the Catholic Church in 1917.

Fashioned after his thoughts, "Thomism" was later recognized as an essential school of thought, not only within the Church but also within secular philosophy. His best known works, all written in Latin, including the theological treatises *Summa contra gentiles* (c. 1258 – 64) and *Summa Theologiae* (1265/66 – 73), which he could not complete before his death on the 7th of March 1274 in Fossanova; commentaries on Aristotle's *De anima - On the Soul -* and *Nichomachean Ethics*; and philosophical works such as *De ente et essentia* (before 1256; *Being and Essence*).

*"**Thomism** is the theology and philosophy of St. Thomas Aquinas (1224/25 – 1274), and it is of various interpretations, usages, and invocations by individuals, religious orders, and schools. Thomism's rich history may be divided into four main periods: the first two centuries after his death (the 14th and 15th centuries), the 16th century, the period from about 1850 to the Second Vatican Council (1962 – 65), and the period from the Second Vatican Council to the present. Aquinas achieved an original synthesis of Aristotelian philosophy and Christian theology. Building upon Aristotle but also making respectful use of the Neoplatonic doctrines of St. Augustine (354 – 430) and the Church Fathers (the bishops and other teachers who expounded orthodox Christianity in the early centuries of the Church), Aquinas developed a distinctive position. He treated existence as the supreme act or perfection of being in God as well as in created things, reserved the creative act to God alone, denied the presence of matter in angels, and thus distinguished between God and created beings by positing that only in created beings is existence distinct from essence. Also characteristic was his teaching that the human soul is a unique subsistent form, substantially united with matter to constitute human nature. Aquinas maintained that the immortality of the human soul can be strictly demonstrated, that there is a real distinction of principles between the soul and its powers of knowing and willing, and that human knowledge is based upon sense experience leading to the mind's reflective activity. He held that both human beings and lower creatures have a natural tendency or love toward God, that supernatural grace perfects and elevates the natural abilities of humans, and that*

blessedness consists formally in knowing God Himself, a knowledge accompanied by full love of God.

This coherent but complex body of Thomistic doctrine was critically examined in the first two centuries after Aquinas's death. In 1273 and again in 1377, aspects of his philosophy were condemned by theologians and bishops and even by the papacy. Most of the issues in question concerned divine knowledge, the relationship between the soul and the body, and Aquinas' understanding of human nature. Aquinas was criticized for making use of Aristotle—whose works had only recently been rediscovered by western European scholars in the wake of the Crusades—and for relying on commentaries on Aristotle, by Muslim philosophers such as Avicenna (980–1037).

The Dominican order, to which Aquinas had belonged, defended his thought, and by 1290 several young teachers were among his strongest advocates. During the 14th century, Aquinas's writings gradually became the standard theological texts of the Dominicans. In the early 15th century, important interpretations and commentaries appeared, including that of the Dominican scholar Jean Capréolus. Capréolus invoked Aquinas to combat the dominant nominalists, who denied the real existence of universals (qualities or properties in virtue of which a class of objects is referred to by the same general term) and gave primacy to the will over the intellect. His Four Books of Defenses of the Theology of Thomas Aquinas (1409–33) inspired numerous other writings by philosophers and theologians drawing mainly from the works of Aquinas. Another Dominican scholar, Antoninus of Florence, discussed in specialized treatises various ethical issues arising from Aquinas's philosophy. Another Florentine

Dominican, the painter Fra Angelico, was influenced by Aquinas's emphasis on the role of emotion in spiritual life and by his insistence on the harmony between nature and grace.

At the University of Salamanca in Spain, Francisco de Vitoria and his successors Domingo de Soto and Domingo Bañez employed a new style of lecturing based directly on Aquinas's greatest work, the Summa Theologiae (1265 or 1266 – 73; "Summary of Theology"). The figures they influenced ranged from the mystic Teresa of Ávila to the defenders of indigenous Americans, notably Barolomé de las Casas. Many of the earliest members of the Jesuit order, including Francisco Toledo and Gregory of Valencia, studied theology at Salamanca under Vitoria, while other important Jesuit thinkers, including Luis de Molina and Francisco Suarez, drew from the teachings of Aquinas to emphasize the activities of human knowledge and freedom.

In Italy, interest in Aristotle and Aquinas continued during the Renaissance. The extensive commentary on the Summa Theologiae by Cardinal Cajetan remains unsurpassed for its detailed analysis. A highly original thinker, Cajetan made his own restatement of the Thomistic arguments. His independence was displayed in his work on the analogy of names, in which he proposed the influential division of kinds of analogy into inequality, attribution, and proportionality, as well as in his opinion that the human soul's immortality can be supported only by probable reasons.

Other noteworthy Dominican commentators in the 16th century were Sylvester of Prierio and Franceso Sylvesteri of Ferrara. The latter's classic commentary on

Aquinas's Summa contra gentiles (c. 1258–64; "On the Truth of the Catholic Faith") showed the importance of this work for the relation of faith and philosophy, the meaning of personhood, and the desire of God.

Thomism's influence began to wane in the 17th century when scholarly interest shifted from dogmatic theology, which concerns Church doctrine, to moral theology, which concerns practical moral principles for everyday life. Nevertheless, dictionaries of Aquinas's ideas and texts and numerous works of apologetics and exposition continued to be published, especially in France, indicating Aquinas's considerable presence in French philosophical scholarship. The Thomist scholars, John of Saint Thomas, Vincent de Contenson, and Charles-René Billuart produced multivolume works in the 17th and 18th centuries. Because Aquinas's pedagogical method of posing and answering theological questions had fallen out of favour, John and subsequent thinkers reorganized Aquinas's writings under thematic categories (e.g., logic, philosophy of nature, and metaphysics). They also juxtaposed Aquinas's works with contemporary meditative texts to make his philosophy appear more relevant to current issues of belief and practice.

Until the mid-19th century, Scholasticism (the philosophical systems of medieval Christian thinkers) and Thomism were little known outside Roman Catholic seminaries. The dominant philosophers of the 17th and 18th centuries, including René Descartes and Immanuel Kant, rejected the medieval foundations of philosophy and theology. From the late 18th century, the school of German idealism, represented by G.W.F. Hegel, Friedrich W.J. von Schelling, and Johann Fichte, eschewed Aquinas's emphasis on natural creation and on the particularity and uniqueness of human nature.

By the middle of the 19th century, Church authorities and some university faculties had become convinced that the Christian faith could be defended against modern idealist and subjectivist philosophies by deploying the realism of Aristotle and Aquinas. In opposition to Hegel's view of reality as the self-realization of "Spirit," they affirmed the stability of aspects of the external world. The renewal of Thomistic thought was advocated by three influential Jesuit writers in Italy and Germany: Luigi Taparelli d'Azeglio, Matteo Liberatore, and Joseph Kleutgen. Their own positions in epistemology, metaphysics, and social theory remained eclectic, but they did give impetus to the work of studying Aquinas and other Scholastics in the light of modern intellectual and social issues.

Decisive support for the movement came with Pope Leo XIII's encyclical Aeterni Patris (1879; "Eternal Father"). It noted the importance of sound doctrine for meeting contemporary problems and called for a restoration of the Christian philosophy of the Church Fathers and Scholastics, augmented where necessary by the reliable advances of modern research. Leo asked especially for a recovery of the wisdom of Aquinas, whom he hailed as "the special bulwark and glory of the Catholic Faith." This programme required an accurate historical study of Aquinas himself and his major commentators, combined with a readiness to use the evidence and resources of modern learning and science. In 1880, Leo made Aquinas patron of all Roman Catholic schools. The Code of Canon Law of 1917, the official compilation of Church laws, required that of philosophy and religion follow the method and principles of Aquinas. This established Thomism as the official philosophy of the Roman Catholic Church.

The Thomistic revival, known as neo-Thomism or the third Thomism (after the Thomism of Aquinas himself and the Thomism of his earlier interpreters), developed in a variety of directions in the first half of the 20th century. The historical studies of Étienne Gilson and Marie-Dominique Chenu on theology in the 12th and 13th centuries enhanced scholarly understanding of Aquinas and his writings. A.D. Sertillanges and Jacques Maritain employed Aquinas's ideas to address modern art, science, and society. Thus, Maritain applied the Thomistic concepts of person and community to the problem of democracy. Several theologians—including Desiré-Joseph Mercirer, Joseph Maréchal, Pierre Rousselot, Catholic teachers Erich Przywara, Ererich Coreth, J.B. Lotz, Karl Rahner, Gustav Siewerth, and Bernard Lonergan—explored potential affinities between Thomism and modern schools of philosophy such as idealism, phenomenology, and existentialism. Other theologians found that Thomism offered a philosophical approach that could serve as an alternative to other medieval or modern schools of thought or as an apologetic response to modern philosophical traditions. One such thinker, Réginald Garrigou-Lagrange, composed defenses of Aquinas's philosophy, commentaries on the Summa Theologiae, and writings on the Christian life.

During the first half of the 20th century, neo-Thomism provided the standard against which every Catholic intellectual movement was measured. Many of its advocates believed that no other way of thinking should be tolerated within the Roman Catholic Church. Unlike the thought of Aquinas, therefore, neo-Thomism in this period was generally rigid and intolerant, overly concerned with logic and metaphysics, and disinterested in the religious depth of Aquinas's writings. What many scholars and theologians referred to as Thomism or neo-Thomism, therefore, was a generic and rather shallow variant of neo-Scholasticism, a contemporary movement also hearkening back to medieval thought but promoting several positions that were contrary to those of Thomas Aquinas.

The Second Vatican Council (Vatican II), which promoted pastoral renewal and greater openness toward non-Western cultures, ended the dismissive attitude of some Roman Catholic thinkers toward non-Thomist theologies. The monopoly exercised by neo-Thomists in the Church collapsed, and Aquinas's influence was reduced. Although the ramifications of Vatican II at first seemed disastrous for Thomism, the council nevertheless provided theologians with ample opportunity to return to the basic principles of Aquinas' theology and to apply them to matters not commonly treated by neo-Thomists. Thomistic concerns that found new expression after Vatican II included the mission of the Holy Spirit, the anticipation of the eschaton (end times), and Christ as the head of the human race. Drawing from themes in Aquinas's theological framework, Roman Catholic thinkers argued that God's grace could be found at work in the seven sacraments, the liturgy, Church ministries, and social movements. Theologians after Vatican II applied Aquinas's insights to medical ethics, Christian virtues, Christian spirituality, and human rights.

In the 1970s new scholarly resources and studies began to appear. In 1974, the seventh centenary of Aquinas's

death, Pope Paul VI issued a commemorative letter; in that same year, a new interest in Aquinas manifested itself in congresses, multivolume collections, computer indices, and centers of Thomistic studies. Major works on Aquinas by Ghislain Lafont, Albert Patfoort, Otto Pesch, Ulrich Horst, S.T. Bonino, and Jean-Pierre Torrell were published in the 1980s and 1990s. These studies, the culmination of the vast research pursued during the 20th century into the historical and religious context of Thomistic thinking, testified to the influence that Aquinas's thought continued to exert in the 20th and 21st centuries".
(Culled from Thomas O'Meara, O. P.; Professor of Theology, Notre Dame University. Author of *Thomas Aquinas Theologian* and others. *https://www.britannica.com /topic/Thomism).*

Let us come back to the involuntary zero net savings at death, which I unequivocally say any person who does not believe in Thomas Aquinas' property rights approaches. Secondly, they may not have any zero net savings at their times of death but they would have negative net savings at death. They have come to believe that the country is only as good as their farm, not as their home; not good enough for their children to live in. At the illegal accumulation of wealth, they send their families to the safe havens abroad and remain sterile, fruitless and accumulate unproductive wealth through stealing and continuous looting in the country, for self-egotism. They buy a lot of choice property at home and abroad, without asking themselves the important question of how long they still have to live in this world that perishes with uses. At their deaths in sins, the financial inflow to their families abroad would decline because changing the Naira into Dollars for foreign exchange transfer is not only a macroeconomic issue, affecting the economy as a whole but also a microeconomic issue, affecting the individual households.

The only phenomenon their families abroad had understood overtime had been cash flowing easily from their fathers' farm to them in Europe and America. So at their deaths, their children would easily sell the property and convert the money from Naira to Dollars, for far less than the amount they were bought years before. The children would give out the property for any amount since the desperation for cash would have become stronger than any father's legacy, till all is finished. That is, if the children would not be killing themselves over their father's will, especially if the man was polygamous, busy sinning with illegal accumulation of women and wealth. Sometimes, children that were never known would resurface at their deaths; solely to struggle for their parts of the illicit wealth. Since they died in sins, they would never see God, to whom they could appeal for forgiveness and restoration of order in the families they left behind.

It may be true that they had already died before their children started killing themselves, and before this negative net savings that is yet to be recognized in economics began to manifest. Who knows whether there is any gain of earthly legacy beyond this world or not, or whether the dead are connected with the happenings in this world or not, as our fathers had said? After all, as we have also read in the Holy Bible, the rich man, in interacting with Abraham, was still concerned about the lifestyles of those he had left behind on his sinful world. I say in his sinful world because the world cannot be a sinful place to the just. Let only he who eats the soured grape have his mouth bent.

I am a Thomist; perhaps a reformed one. I hold the opinion that it is an arrogance of wealth for a man to build houses he does not need, and are not available for others' use. When I see friends discussing the latest models of cars they already own, I call it ostentation and smugness. When I see friends who use cars to decorate their compounds, even some antiquities, as if they have no relatives, or that all their friends and relatives are already well off, I call it arrogance of wealth and sins against humanity. It does not matter whether the wealth is legitimately acquired or not. This is because such bliss in wicked and primitive accumulation is part of the weakness and paleness of the flesh, as it neglects the reason for God's given wealth. When I hear the unnecessary acquisitions of luxuries like private jets, even by men of God, I call such barren achievements. Are these resources wasted on these luxuries, not more than enough to make Nigeria a "good place to be born in, especially if the Thomistic two property rights; the right of acquisition and the right of usage are practiced? Those waste products of the rich are more than enough lifelines for the poor. They are enough to enable the poor speedily pass through the initial obstacles of development. The poor, at least, need the so called waste resources of the rich, "as an aircraft needs a critical minimum speed to become airborne". Perhaps the rich need to understand that "poverty anywhere is a threat to prosperity everywhere". So that the new economic order that places obligations on the rich to support the poor is not solely on the interests of the poor.

Nevertheless, every child of the country is being infested with different behavioural syndromes, so that one would be very wrong to think that only the politicians are wicked. During my course of studies, I have encountered a university Professor who would recommend up to eight textbooks for his students without his real basic text. He would keep that very far away from them; just to practice his wickedness of setting the questions that he would be unable to answer, and without changing a word or a figure in his questions since he would also copy the answers from the book. Sometimes, he would deliberately set the questions that have double barreled answers; say, Alternative "A" or Alternative "B", with either of them being correct but with only him to decide the correct answers to his questions. Should he have any of his students he wants to injure – he always had - and be happy that someone is sad, he would wait for the examination to be written before drawing the marking scheme with Alternative "B", if the student's answer is with Alternative "A" or he allots higher marks to what his "student enemy" did not write, vice visa. After all, in the event of any protest by the student, it is the marking scheme he would be asked to produce; and no student is allowed to question another student's grade.

Whereas a teacher is supposed to have utmost good faith with his students and see them as his most important assets, he would happily celebrate his student's failure. That is more than bullying, but also terrorism. Isn't it? In this case of such extreme wickedness and terrorism, the Professor must die for his students to live, to be free and to be happy. There is no way he can make heaven, except he repents. He alone is the teacher living in his sinful world, not with another who has utmost good faith with his students. Anyway, I do not ever regard him as one of my teachers; I cannot even remember what I learnt from him.

I must tell the story with nostalgia what we did to him in one of our postgraduate examinations; doctoral examination to be specific. We got his hidden book from which he usually set his questions verbatim, after we had failed his first examination. We nicknamed him after the author of his hidden book and resolved to solve and memorize all the alternatives answers in the book without bothering to understand anything since we were in emergency situation. We had to go into hiding in a venue very far away from the faculty building, in case there was a bird that could whistle the information in his ears, and we excluded the students we suspected could give him the information. True to our calculation that he would not change any word and figure given his past questions, his examination appeared to us like placing salt before the goat. We did not even need to read and understand any of the questions because we had mastered them in our tutorials. We answered each question with all the possible alternatives, using "or", because he fell into our trap.

When the scripts were passed to him (much later), he rejected them, promoting that the examination was not properly invigilated by the younger lecturers who was so assigned. He insisted that we would rewrite the examination. At that point, the radical tendency inside me once again forced its way out even though I had tried, by the pieces of advice from some of the Professors who knew how to prepare my 'mental health medicines' (my second supervisor was foremost among them, and I specially have him to thank for my success in the programme), to calm down. I threatened heavily to gather all our tutorial papers as evidence to petition the University Senate that he has been involved in plagiarism. I encouraged my colleagues not to be afraid but to take their lives in their hands, and since it was between pass or fail for everybody at a doctoral paper, which would once again make some of us miss another qualifying comprehensive examination to the thesis stage, they easily went with me. Some, including me, were not writing the particular paper for the first time with some up to the third time, and his was the only examination that I ever failed in the whole of my schooling life (from Primary School to my Doctorate Level).

As I late heard, one of his colleagues in the department quickly informed him of my threat and advised him accordingly. The next day, he quickly released the result with obvious annoyance, with a "C" grade for all of us. That became his problem because a "C" grade was good enough to proceed to the next stage in a doctoral programme. After all, it was a terminal examination. He was lucky anyway, because I would have definitely carried out my threat without mercy. I would have sued if the University Senate had failed to do something about it, God knew that. In short my "crazy" Lawyer (friend) was already waiting. He has those my medicine makers to thank.

Besides his attitude to his students, he has no respect for his colleagues who he believes are all inferior to him. He would come to class and attempt to talk down his colleagues before the student. How he came about this belief is something that flummoxes everybody. He has not done anything extra-ordinary as an academic; he has not won any international grant or award to the department where grant masters abounds. He has not written a single book in a department that has authors who are read across many Nigerian universities and beyond. He has not been head of any agency or work outside the university system and brings honours to a department that can boast of former Director Generals and United Nation/ African Commission consultants. He has not been called upon as a political office holder or as a keynote or guest speaker in any international conference form a department that has seasoned resource persons. He keeps boasting of being an undergraduate of the Nigerian premier university nearly four decades ago, bending his head and closing his eyes while walking as if the head is loaded with too much knowledge, whereas his department has a Summa Cum Laude graduate from one of the Ivy League schools, many American Universities graduates with many of his younger colleagues as African Economic Research Consortium scholars. Yet, such a local man sees himself better than everyone else; terrible! It only accidentally happened that we are of the same Esan tribe, if he does not see himself as too much to be an Esan man.

CHAPTER SIX

Like the Children of Israel

Nigerians were just like the children of Israel, to whom God had given a king for their prosperity but who rejected God's ordained king and yelled for another king according to their wisdom. Like He did to the children of Israel, God allowed us, Nigerians our wish of a king, in this case, the President, and Baba Bubu came upon us all. God had always allowed humans their freewill and determinism. When the president we had preferred to God's began to bite us with scorpions, some of us could no longer say something was wrong, at least not immediately. They began to pretend that they were enjoying the bites, even when they were dying. They just started admitting that it has never been so bad, but that appears too late in the day. Most painful is that some of those who for their selfish reasons put the people in this problem had died and gone away with it; without apology and repentance. It is painful that they left with the stain because I believe they will not make heaven. What will they tell the angels at the blissful gate? What will they tell God?

Goodluck Ebele Jonathan, herein referred to as President Jana for the love I have for him, the immediate past president of Nigeria, was a very meek man who understood that power comes only from God. He may have had his faults – meekness and kindness to a fault - but those are the infallibilities of humans. Of course, he did has his faults even with his people and offended his party men and women, especially that he did not fragmentize or polarize the country as his predecessor has done. President Jona as the number one citizen of the country believed that from the east to the west, from the north to the south, Nigeria was first and foremost to be considered in his heart and decision making. So, his ambition did not worth the blood of any Nigerian; not even the blood of the "useless" mad man in the street. On the contrary, his predecessor believes that only a part of the north is his constituency and that his ambition and that of his tiny ethnic group are worth the blood of as many people as possible, even the most important scientists in the land. He has so far succeeded and would go scotch free with it. Instead of him being incarcerated to pay for his sins, he would incarcerate Nigerians of goodwill and gets paid his severance and his pension for life; for destroying the country.

However, the people called President Jona's attitude in power weakness. This is because so many of them had not seen a meek president for a long time, in short, in their lives. It is not our culture to have a meek leader; for we call such weak. The more a governor issues threats to his people or his political party leaders, the more we believe that he is a tough leader. In short, his followers would urge him on; to show that there cannot be two governors in the state, as the governor is the leader of the party in the state, and it is the periods of such crises those followers profit from.

The reason for this is very clear; the country's democracy was still somehow nascent during President Jona's regime. The Military had ruled us for a long time with highhandedness, promulgating obnoxious decrees and forcing the citizens to breathe, and in all manners of draconian behaviour. So, we have inherited wars from among ourselves. Toughness by threats and dictatorship, not by performance has become our portion. It would then be hard to accept that a leader could be meek, soft, empathizing, sympathizing, and also be regarded as tough.

Baba Obasara, the first of the this republic, as I said before, is arguable the best since his immediate successor, who was sincere and largely sympathetic with poor Nigerians' conditions, did not live long enough to be evaluated. I say so because presidents normally show their true colours around the fifth year in office. President Baba Bubu is an exemption; he did not wait a minute because as the Esan maxim has it, it does not take any time and anything for a woman who has always wanted to cry in public to display her tears. However, Baba Obasara was of a military background and could match the military styles of ruling the people by force, with Nigeria's constitution as the problem he wished could be set aside. Perhaps, he was simply the best of his time, because none among his peers could have easily been bold to disorganize those facets of the military and dislodge them from the political arena, which has to do with the plotting of coups. Baba Obasara helped us to retire all the political soldiers to formally become politicians, instead of nursing the ambitions to steal power. He did not retire those from the far north and left those from his North West zone, as Baba Bubu has been fond of doing. This Baba Obasara's action is a great legacy, and no one is expected to ask how or why.

Nevertheless, as I had said, it was also he, who cracked the kernel that the fowl has swallowed, since he was foremost among Nigerians who betrayed the Nigerians' goodwill by bringing Baba Bubu upon the people. He may have been tempted to be joined in it because of the unwarranted and unhealthy competition with President Jona; on who would become the longest serving president of Nigeria, as if there would be any Nobel Prize Robert Mugabe of Zimbabwe could not win for that feat. I guess it was this ambition that required him to quickly crack the kernels on his knees, as he could not wait for the children to bring the diminutive rock reserved for that purpose. With his damaged knees, how would he now trek to the market to sell the oil produced from the kernels? That is very difficult.

In essence, the people were experiencing a truly democratic president for the first time under President Jana. The people were not used to his simple styles and as such, the styles galled them. Perhaps he inherited the work attitude from his immediate predecessor in office or that they were only birds of the same feathers. The latter must be the case. For example, he refused to crack down on the press or arrest journalists and authors who wrote widely, and some falsely against him. As the most abused president on the pages of newspapers in the history of the country, he did not set any journalist up for death and claimed that he died in the hands of a hit and run driver. As the

Commander-in-Chief, he refused to order the military to demolish villages in the name of fighting crimes and simply called the many innocent souls that would have been sent to their untimely graves "collateral damage". In his own village, many people who were against a man of humble beginning becoming the President of the country were allowed to move freely in the street without molestations. There was a time some poor people under the umbrella of a religious sect in the north blocked the road and attempted to attack his convoy, and he did not order the military to clear out the dissidents. He did not brand genuine agitators terrorists and simply turned them into terrorists indeed. He did not order one 'Operation Tortoise Fly' or one 'Operation Crocodile Laugh' or one "Snake Dace" to "decisively deal with" and kill human beings made by God in His image.

These and many more did not go down well with even some of his party men, who believed that his extreme gentility in handling issues in the country made them to lose power to the opposition. It was truly a factor because Nigerians had become so gullible to those who survive by tricks and intrigues, and since he did not want that kind of life style, he was on his own Then, unlike an African leader, he simply ensured a transition of power from himself as president to a man who defeated him in a controversial election. His political party members whose families were in the safe haven abroad, wanted him to use his incumbency to abuse the electoral process and allow the blood of innocent people to flow. He maintained that his ambition did not worth the blood of any man. Those party men had long become parts of the Nigerian problem, as they could not just stay in where peace and progress reign. They have since joined Baba Bubu and his cohort since they could not afford to stay out of government for even a short period. They are capitalists without businesses. They have no productive occupations or businesses to maintain their synthetic and affluent life styles outside government. In such a case, they are the ones being referred to in the Esan adage, which says the heat of the sun has separated the void shells of melon seeds from the fecund ones.

Well, I know why this is so. I have narrated it somewhere before. When this republic was about to be birthed by Gen Abdulsalami Abubakar, herein referred to as Baba Abdul for the love I have for him, so many decent persons stayed back and watched from afar because of the ugly past in the country's democratic journey. This became so in the experience of the democratic journey midwifed by Gen. Ibrahim Babagida, herein referred to as Baba Maradona for the love I have for him. However, I must be careful to do posterity a favour to remark that for this consistent refusal to return the country to a democratic rule till he was forced to "step aside" from his "government of settlements", Baba Maradona would have been among the best presidents Africa ever had. Maybe destiny never wanted it that way.

This lack of trust by decent and busy people that Baba Abdul would hand over within the few months he promised gave the thugs, who after all, had nothing to lose should the military not truly hand over power to the civilians, the chance to occupy the political arena. Since then, they have looted the country dry and have become so powerful amid uneducated and impoverished citizens that till now, they dictate the way things should go. They have been able to entrench a government of crude personalities and coarsed culture all over the country. They have made nothing but indecency reigns supreme. That is why any decent human being irritates them as rude and "a holy, holy man". That is why they do not understand and trust sane and just reasoning people. That is why people with good education are always threats to them. They can only bring forth their kinds.

What sort of a Nigerian president would allow peaceful protests to hold, no matter how mega and would beg protesters that their grievances would be addressed by the government? This, President Jona continued to do without reminding the electorates that they cannot intimidate his government? What sort of a Nigerian president would allow freedom of speech on national televisions, and writings by authors against him? Why did he not close down television stations and harass journalists and authors with the security agencies? Then, the security agencies that could not control simple vices or could not arrest a burglar of the President's house in the very seat of power are being made to harass innocent citizens.

There was a time President Jona named one of the most prestigious universities in the country after a sacrificial lamp of our democracy. It was highly resisted by the students of the university who were either not born or too young to understand the sacrifice. There were other politicians who either never liked the lamp or did not want President Jana to take the glory, and thus incited the young ones against it. As a democratic president, he tactically withdrew the idea to give peace a chance, instead of simply closing down the university and ordering the military to shoot at sight, any student who dared to voice his opposing views, as a typical Nigeria Commander-in-Chief would do

– like in the case of the #EndSARS protest. Baba Bubu would arrest all those who could be arrested; just to send the message that his government is not ready to tolerate any protest, and by implication, not ready for democracy. He sees any protest as trying to remove him. So he was told by the cabal. It is when it comes to the armless civilians that his fist usually becomes a big bunch, to the extent of ordering the arrest of innocent cats because of his delusory belief that the leader of a protest in the South-West has some magical powers of transmuting into a cat to invade arrests. What a shame? It showed that magical powers are in the veins of his cabal and they think all of us like themselves.

Baba Bubu has not heard of how his counterpart and fellow dictator in Chad had died in the battle front defending his country – since he liked wars anyway. He did not hear of how Muammar Gadaffi had refused to go into exile and preferred to fight and die in Libya to give his people peace – since he would not let power go anyway. By extension, he did not hear that the great Madiba was not afraid to be honourable by dying in a South African hospital instead of wasting his country's resources to be surviving at the mercy of doctors in a United Kingdom hospital. He only remembers that he was once a soldier when it comes to dealing ruthlessly with armless civilians who dare to criticize him or demand self-determination – treating the symptoms instead of treating the disease, and thus, fuelling it.

Baba Bubu's spokesmen may have succeeded in quickly telling us off; doing everything possible to tell the world that nobody died from the shootings of the #EndSARS protest, but not that there were no shootings. Nobody died or injured in where there were sporadic shootings of heavy guns with live bullets by soldiers! What was the need for the shooting at armless protesters, wasting the bullets that could not kill or cause injuries to criminals? Are these not parts of the common resources that should have been targeted at terrorists, even if at best, no fly was injured in that protest? Are the sounds of guns shots and humans so compatible that obedient citizens who were waving the country's flag had to be threatened with guns just because they expressed their views? A Senior Advocate of Nigeria could heartlessly show himself in national television defending the government, telling the country people that morality has no place in law. Whether Baba Bubu likes it or not, the #ENDSARS protest and the massacre of youths therefrom have become disgusting events of history in Nigeria. Generations yet unborn would commemorate its centennials (anniversaries) in extraordinary ways. Yet, some others would mourn it eternally. The story would be continuously told of how the government of Baba Bubu had turned a peaceful protest into a violent demonstration and took the opportunity to kill innocent youths who only expressed themselves, with their corpses never recovered. It does not matter who is hired to defend the President now. By that time, none of us born now would be alive anymore but it would become the only event Baba Bubu would be remembered for.

Baba Bubu did not hear that American soldiers came all the way just to rescue one of their 'ordinary citizens' from a terrorists' den at his backyard and without him as the President knowing what happened. He leads a country where bandits can be so free to, and rampantly kidnap students from both secondary and tertiary educational institutions, even from a moving train. Where else have we heard that? Whenever the news of killings of students is broken, the presidency, not even the President, would simply release a press statement, mourning the students. They would, as usual, vow in their empty manners to the winds, to deal with the situation. Then, with the emergence of all kinds of insecurity in the land, the government would not agree that something is wrong. The President's hit men still painfully insult Nigerians' intelligence that he is the best president in Nigerian history – for a so bad administration that is obvious to the blind and audible to the deaf. His men would want to summarize it; that terrorism is a world problem, which had also happened in America. This is referring the people to the about two decade ago September Eleven attack of the World Trade Centre in the United States of America. They would not ask themselves how often it has happened there since then or whether such events have had any high incidence and wide prevalence in United States of America or not.

His very disreputable and notorious Minister of Information would stand on top of the roof shouting that Nigeria is calm, safe, and secured, with the President incapable of knowing what is going on. It is a shameful performance from a shameless president of a country. Prof. Wole Soyinka, herein referred to as The Prof, for the love I have for him, once asked them to remove their useless pride and seek help. But the President's semi-illiterate Assistants easily wave off the words of the only Nobel Prize Winner in Nigeria, as the words of a mad man. What a paradox?

For me as a person, Baba Bubu has not disappointed me because in the first place, I was not one of those who expected anything good from him. Even if he succeeds with his dearly beloved Rural Grazing Area or Water Bill or National Livestock Transformation, in any guise to aid the Fulani agenda of occupying Nigeria, there would always be National and State Assemblies. There would always be agitations for successions in an unjust society even if he succeeds in exterminating the duo of Nnamdi Kanu and Sunday Igboho, herein referred to as Mazi and Otunba respectively, for the love I have for them. One day, sooner than expected, a debtor would be forced to pay his creditor and everybody would know who Allah gave which land.

Did President Jona use even hot water to disperse the popular #OccupyNigeria protesters, let alone Baba Bubu himself, who was part of that historic protest? When Baba Bubu called for the monkeys and the baboons to be soaked in blood simply because the people were yet to vote for him, he was not arrested. The #EndSARS protest was the most peaceful protest and the hope of Nigerian youths until the government began to sponsor their thugs and hoodlums to counter the protesters, thereby causing violence. It was the same thing the government wanted to do at the venue of #HarassBabaBubu out of London, organized by the modern Revolutionist, Reno Imokri, herein referred to as Reno, for the love I have for him, but they forgot that London was not Nigeria.

What if Baba Bubu had not won the election that brought him in as the President of Nigeria? Or better put; what if the peaceful President Jona had refused to accept defeat in the face of glaring evidence of unfairness in that election? Baba Bubu would have certainly burnt down the country, as the monkeys and the baboons would have once again been soaked in blood, in line with his vow, all in the name of a ringed election against the chief patron of all the extremist groups put together. Yet, as he has won, the monkeys and the baboons are still being soaked in blood for resisting the Fulani agenda. Or do we think that it was only accidental that he has to appoint a sympathizer with terrorist groups as key Ministers in the country? Nigerians wanted the President to sack a terrorist sympathizer from his cabinet, forgetting that, as the African adage goes, striking remembrance will never allow the fowl to swallow the eggs of the bird.

Those who continued to blame President Jona for handing over to a known bigot should understand that the country was between the devil and the deep blue sea, or between two margins of self-survival. The country should pass through this unfortunate stage, survive it, and its citizens become wiser, if ever, than endless blood bathes in the country, and by extension, within the West African sub-region. Those who were to be blamed were the many influential elites who combined to bring Baba Bubu upon Nigerians, but most of whom have apologized. President Jona as the President must have been privileged to information the rest of his political party men were not. He had promised not to sacrifice anybody for power and the only way to be his own man was to trade off power to avoid violence and blood in the streets. In any case, an election was conducted; one in which he participated. So, however anybody felt, he had no option than to be smaller than the law and the country. He simply did the right thing.

CHAPTER SEVEN

Who Would Rescue Them?

I have still not fully answered the question of what would have happened if Baba Bubu had not come to power and I do not think that I can exhaust it. It is now difficult to see any person who agrees that he voted for him; not even the plenty "Say Baba" wheelbarrow pushers are proud of him anymore. He only succeeded in using his tiny kinsmen to threaten his predecessor to surrender to him. Unable to fulfill his "occupy Nigeria agenda" promise to his ethnic group, he has made the rest citizens, who once appreciated them as fellow Nigerians, their enemies. It was never thought that the Fulani people in Nigeria were so few; for it was never known to the people of the south that the majority of the Hausa people in the north are not Fulani people. Who would rescue them when Baba Bubu, who had set a tall and frustrating target for them, and abandoned them at the middle of the fight, finally leaves power? Who would help to reintegrate them and withdraw the debauched impressions already sown in the minds of the people that their only ambition is to occupy any part of Nigeria by force? Who would make them friends of their fellow citizens again, as it was in the days before Baba Bubu, when they were not seen as killers? It was a delight for the villagers to meet the herdsmen and their cows on the bush paths to the farms. As children, we used to have many sweet nursery rhymes for them and the governors did not have any need enacting anti-open grazing laws?

It was not the first time a man from the Fulani ethnic tribe had become the President of the country. Yet, ever since, the fires in them were geared towards productivity. The people in the south saw 'herdsmen", not the now "Fulani herdsmen", as harmless. They did not willfully lead their cows to eat up any community residents' farms. They did not rape women, and kill people by the authority of their patron president of the country. The people brought them to their houses whenever they were homeless, instead of allowing them to perpetually live in the bushes. There was no need for such thing as banning open grazing because they were neither incited to deliberately graze their cows on the crops of the farmers nor use their AK-47 guns on humans. If they had guns before Baba Bubu started the incitements, and subsequently became the President of the country, the guns were for wide animals, which they gladly shared with their host communities.

As I already said, Umoru Yar'dua, another Fulani man was a president of the country in this dispensation, and these carnages by the Fulani herdsmen never happened. It only took a bigot; a man with a bitter heart in power, to attract them from wherever they were and release the criminalities in them, thereby attracted hatred to them. It is now safer to first of all assume that any momentous crime committed in any community is by the Fulani herdsmen.

If the Fulani's benefactor; the "true Fulani" Baba Bubu - for those Fulani men who do not key into their land conquering agenda are not true Fulani men - had wanted to help them, would he had waited for the governors to be making laws banning open grazing before doing something to help his people? Would he ever allow his children and grandchildren to take to such primitive occupation in the 21st century? Did he not know how he had developed his ranch? As the President, he could have acquired large acres in the different willing regions of the country and beyond, lease or donate such lands to his poor kinsmen for ranching. He could insist that the Central Bank of Nigeria gives them zero-interest loans – which would never have been paid back anyway - or grants for the cow business.

If the willing regions are only in the north, then, the business of cows would become even more lucrative to his kinsmen, because portions of beef are more consumed in the south. All they would need was to buy the green pastures for cow consumptions from the south, just as the south buy onions and tomatoes for human consumptions from them. After all, there was the proposal of importing glasses from Brazil to feed cows, and by the same president who had placed a ban on the importations of rice that feed human beings. Nigerian youths too, northerners or southerners, would have lucrative businesses of buying grasses from the south and selling them as inputs to ranches in the north. A youth can bring onions or tomatoes to the south and carry grasses back to the north with a lot of profit margin. That would mean that the north produce cows for the consumption in the south, and as usual, the producers become richer, at least, in this sub-sector. Would that not be better than inciting the northern traders' strikes; to refuse to sell onions and tomatoes in the south? Would it not be truer that they feed the nation than the empty threats of strikes in which nobody except the producers of the perishable goods are losers? Assuming without conceding that the south cannot produce onions, and then the north refuse to sell onions to the south, is there anywhere the nutritionists have written that nobody can function without onions? If the green houses in the south are unable to sufficiently produce them, the Burkinabes' traders would be glad to flood Lagos markets with onions, tomatoes and beans.

This ranching policy would not add to the cost of rearing cows because it takes more to transport live cows than to move grasses from one region to the other, let alone moving them from bush to bush and taking care of their health needs; and many times, all these are done at the risks of accidents and dangerous reptiles. This means it would only be for the purpose of marketing cows would be moved from the north to the south. This is better than the President making cow business a national project and his kinsmen national enemies. Many further innovations would emerge from the many agricultural value chain. If only the President knew that policy is the only instrument that can enable a nation or a region overcome its disadvantage destiny in the development matrix.

It is just that Baba Bubu and his cohort are haters, bitterer and are interested in land conquests wars in the name of grazing cows. Otherwise, it would have been a win-win situation for the north and the south. He has only called his kinsmen to war, laying a heavy burden on their shoulders while he and his family members, who reside and school abroad are not prepared to touch the burden with their fingers. He had thought that he could use them to execute some ancient and primordial Fulani motives in Nigeria. Those motives were dead on arrival; they can merely wobble around as long as the bigot reigns. Not even the "non-true Fulani" or the enlightened Fulani would believe and support the idea that Allah has given them all the lands in Nigeria; something the first tribe to enter into the country has not claimed. Not even the progenitors of the Fulani would have believed that in this age. Then, where did Allah wants the rest of us who are far more in number, to live in?

CHAPTER EIGHT

President Mohammadu Baba Bubu's Supporters

Baba Bubu's supporters would not have allowed the citizens of the country have a breathing space if he had not become the President. They would have caused whoopla everywhere that the Naira would have been at par with the Dollar and that Nigeria would have long left the group of import dependent countries, just as homegrown foods would have been in surplus. They would hoopla that a bag of the most staple foodstuff, rice, would have been fifty percent cheaper than it was in 2014. They would make a ballyhoo that a bag of cement would have crashed to the extent that housing for all would not have remained a myth. They would razzmatazz everywhere that insecurity would have been a thing of the past. There would have been serious hullaballoo about manufacturing that would have been the country's hallmark. There would have been uproars about all the roads that would have been asphalted.

They would cause commotion on electricity that would have long been fixed; within six months from his swearing in as president, with twenty four hours of power supply all over the country. They would have yelled about the country's Gross Domestic Product that would have been growing steadily at more than ten percent per annum despite any global recession(s). They would have so exaggerated Nigerian youths' condition who would have been gainfully employed, and those on voluntary unemployment for education and training who would have been getting monthly stipends steadily. They would have embellished all the bad hospitals that would have long become mega and so equipped with the latest technologies, transforming the health sector that no Nigerian would have experienced the "failure of success hypothesis". Medical tourism abroad would have strictly been prohibited for political office holders or at least, rendered very unattractive, starting from the President himself.

Students would have been on scholarships and university campuses would have been places to behold, while the lecturers would have become the highest paid in Africa and among the highest paid in the world, with no reason to contemplate any strike. The country would have long recovered from her brain losses, as Diaspora Nigerians would have long been encouraged to return home to contribute their quotas to the development of the country. Brain drain would have been arrested, as nobody would have been interested in leaving the country anymore, leaving the embassies with the only option of community developments, if they still wanted to remain relevant. The country would have been far more united by now, and it would have long been zero level of indiscipline. The list could go on and on. Above all, corruption, which Baba Bubu and his co-travelers had thought was an economic policy, would have long been out of the Nigeria's dictionary because Mr. Integrity had come to tear the page out.

They have known better now because they had no singular clue of how the economy works. As if to tell President Jona well done, they tried to woo him into their failure and to use the carefully selected members of his cabinet for rebranding their failure in one way or the other. Even the President has surrendered his party to the opposition members who had worked with President Jona, so long they are willing to cross over, as all top national officers of his party now, including the Chairman and Secretary were President Jona's men. That is how much they have come to understand that unease lies the head that wears the crown. Again, that is a little too late and a little too small.

However today, Nigerian currency is among the poorest in Africa, both in nominal and real terms. A Hundred Naira note now behaves like the Ten Naira note of 2014 and a Thousand Naira note now behaves like the Two Hundred Naira note of 2014. The country has become more and more import dependent, as it has resorted more and more to the outdated style of protectionism. What we have is sectional closures of the borders, because we have become the skeptics - afraid to compete with the rest of the world in the unprecedented waves of globalization that are already here with us, in which no one country can do anything about than initiate policies to reap from its advantages – following the hyperglobalists and the transformationists schools of thought.

Hence, Nigeria has almost been isolated from the rest of the world and living in a state of autarky. At inauguration, the President did not think of searching for high profiled Nigerian at home and abroad to help the country compete, as Baba Obasara and President Jona had done in a person of the World Bank renowned economist, Ngozi Okonjo-Iweala, herein referred to as Dr. Ngoo Dogood for the love I have for her. My kinsman, Arch. Mike Oziegbe Onolememmen, herein referred to as Dr. Bulldozer for the love I have for him, and others too numerous to mention here, were some of them. And because they did not want to associate with any discovering of Baba Obasara and President Jona, they had tried hard in vain to rubbish Dr. Ngoo Dogood's achievements in government, only to find themselves, according to the African adage, to be using their mouths to gulp on their rumps when the rest of the world once again recognized her. More annoying was that those who could neither produce their elementary school certificates nor mention the names of their elementary schools had the effrontery to open their wide mouths to criticize the economic policies of a world renowned economist. Indeed, it is a country where horses can fly.

Instead of being patriotic, swallow their pride and beg Dr. Ngoo Dogood and the likes of Prof. Soludo, herein referred to as Prof. Solution for the love I have for him, to help out, the government went to hire one small girl whose highest qualification is a higher diploma without any known contact. Her job was to complete the job which a doctorate degree holder and thoroughly bred professional had started. Yet, they expected results. In the same way, they made one analogue 'Baba' to take over from such a highly qualified and thoroughly bred professional, Dr. Akinwumi Adesina, hereby referred to as Dr. Adeade for the love I have for him, in the Ministry of Agriculture and expected results.

Dr. Ngoo Dogood had singlehandedly ensured that Nigeria's debts, which have mounted again were forgiven. She ensured that the Dollar was kept in check, even in the face of falling oil prices in the global market. Nigerians saw, though only recognized later, what it meant to manage an economy.

When Baba Bubu and his weak men took over power, they met all the policies that attracted foreign investors and ensured the continuous inflows of foreign exchange into the country. However, they saw all the policies as corruption and voided them with fiats. In less than six months, over Eighty Six Billion United States Dollars flew out of the country in their very eyes. They also created so much tension in the country that even the "bull" would not think of allowing his investments to remain in Nigeria any longer, let alone the "bear" coming in. With Dollars flying out of the country on daily basis but unnoticed by them, the forces of demand and supply sooner came to play and the Naira, now far more in supply, and with increased demand for the Dollar, continued to depreciate.

Yet, they would never own up to their incompetence so that those who could help them may do so. Instead, they have continued to strive in blame games, propaganda, and falsehoods; the only jobs the infamous Minister of Information appears to have been hired to teach the rest of them. Anyway, it is no longer possible for things to be remedied in the lifetime of the administration. We are already in a very bad situation, which we have to endure to the end. The big hope is that the moment the administration is over, the next president would not need to do much before the country would bounce back, because the development partners would be happy to return, especially if the next government is formed by a different political party.

Meanwhile, the activities of the parallel marketers were not checked but allowed to be worsened, because those in government do not understand the concept of price administration in elementary economic theory. They do not understand that whenever any administrative policy to enforce price floor - a maximum price above which goods cannot be sold, is emplaced, parallel markets would spring up. Thus, the price of a bag of rice is so more than tripled that new knowledge from economists is needed to explain this type of inflation in the Nigerian stagflation economy. The unprecedented depreciation of the local currency has already affected almost the price of every item in the market since Nigeria is an import dependent country, importing inflations. Yet, the government still went ahead to place embargos on the necessities of life. What a crazy idea? Someone in government with very limited knowledge of economics must have told them that china did so. Did they need an elementary economics teacher to tell them that no one bans what his people have not produced and still avoid deadweights and albatrosses to progress?

Next, was that the same set of people started exonerating themselves and tagging the poor woman who increased the price of her locally produced *garri* greedy. They ignorantly continue to argue that it was not their policy that led to the increase in the prices of rice and other staple foods in the market but the greed of the citizens, otherwise, why would the price of *garri,* not being imported or affected by the Dollars also increase? They argue. They are not expected to know the relevance of simultaneous equations modeling in economics, or what the market interactions are all about. However, if the President were an erudite man or at least, what Nigerian youths call "correct man", sycophants would not have been able to convince him with such reckless statements that Nigerians were greedy. And because he is not a "correct man", and his Ministers are either on their own or did not also know enough, he did not realize that there are so many interactions in the product market. The interactions are such that increases in the prices of locally produced goods will follow the currency ordained depreciation because the woman who is producing *garri* does not consume only the *garri* she produces; she would also need to buy rice. So, if she must maintain near the level of utility as in the previous periods, she has to raise the price of her *garri* to be able to buy rice at the new high price. This is so because she is a rational producer and consumer who is forced to amend her household economy. She would not survive the new hash reality as a moralist. I chose to use this partial analysis between the *garri* and rice sellers for simple illustration. This holds in the general analysis.

CHAPTER NINE

My Short Presentation

For the avoidance of doubt, below is a short presentation I made as a debate panelist on inflation and sundry issues in my dream concerning Nigeria:

"Introduction

There are five major goals of macroeconomics, and the third of them is price stability - curbing inflation. Where there are good economic managers, inflation should not exceed single digit, as opposed to the current 18.7% and over 30% for goods and food items respectively in Nigeria today and still rising. Managers of the Nigerian economy do not probably know that most of the goals are antagonistic to one another, the reason why many policies often crash or summersault on them. Surely, the Nigerian economy has never been so bad in decades, especially with runaway inflation co-existing with high unemployment rate - stagflation.

A *Brief Review of the Issues*

In the recent past, before 2015, the country was able to record an appreciable level of growth while at the same time keeping inflation in check. In this particular case of inflation bedeviling Nigeria, it negates or truncates the simple Philip Curve, which tells us that inflation has a trade-off with unemployment. However, while inflation is rising in Nigeria, unemployment is also rising. Nothing can be worse; if a country is not at least, better off with one. It was not so in the past. Therefore, the current state of the economy is not only bad but also precarious.

The real problem(s) facing Nigerian economy now is dated back to the built up tensions to the 2015 general elections, and the inexperienced managers who thereafter took over what was an emerging economy. This is not to say that there were no problems at all in the Pre-2015 eras.

Both Baba Obasara's and President Jona's administrations had good foci. There were mixtures of both foreign trained and homegrown intelligentsias to manage the economy. This almost led to the attractions of the Akamutsu's "Flying Geese", with capital on their wings to, identify Nigeria as a good place to perch and even lay their golden eggs. Nigeria made policies that could help overcome the disadvantages of our destiny in the development matrix and gradually lead to industrialization.

Firstly, was to compete favourably in the globalization process, because no country lives under autarky anymore. Foreign exchange flew in either through the sales of crude oil or through participation in the world financial politics. This Dr. Ngoo Dogood did so well, using both her knowledge and contacts with the big players in the world economic and financial markets. Then, we reaped, to a large extent, the advantages of the world's interconnectedness.

Secondly, carrots were placed before the development partners for foreign exchange. The importance of foreign exchange inflow stems from the import dependency of the Nigerian economy. It meant that not too much Naira were purchasing too few dollars. So, we managed to keep the value of the local currency moderately stabilized, and importers did not have to import inflations into the country.

The Present Nigeria's Economic Woes

Then came the Baba Bubu's administration, in which pseudo economists thought that corruption was an economic policy came in. They did not know how much of the campaign against corruption should be done, or how much of it should even be tolerated in the corruption-development equation, in order not to jeopardize the progress already made. They canceled all the incentive or carrot policies designed to attract the world's big players (remember that they are not Father Christmas). Foreign Direct Investors left the country to neighboring countries but our economic managers did not have a clue of what was going on.

Available data showed that within six months, over $U.S.86billion flew out of the country. Naira became so depreciated like never before, as the Dollar skyrocketed, due to the forces of demand and supply in the currency market, and importers had to sell according to the prices of *the Dollars with which they imported their goods – importing inflation. For example, the price of the most staple food, rice skyrocketed and more than doubled. Upon this, there was ban this and ban that, all the border closures.*

Whereas protectionism is not appealing any longer, we closed borders against even what we had not produced and cannot produce, increasing our citizens' deadweights (losses). As it is with policies of price administration, black markets also emerged here and there for the ban items. These illegal markets were not checked either because the Custom Service too wanted to report high revenue generations or because of corruption.

Due to product market interactions, locally produced food items followed in the direction of price rise. For example, a woman producing garri would not only consume her garri, she needs to buy rice and since the price of rice has increased, she has to increase her garri if she must attain near her previously attained utility level, because she is, though not an oriental economist, tailoring her household economy. Morality will not feed her family.

On Money Printing

I had written that increased money supply or expansionary monetary policy is one of the monetary policies (instruments) of the apex bank. I had also said that I had no data to evaluate the particular one under scrutiny, based on the alarm raised by Gov. Godwin Obaseki, herein referred to as Mr. Godwinner for the love I have for him. However, having heard from the Minister of Budget and Planning, I concluded that the Central Bank of Nigeria only took instruction from the executive arm of government to print money, without following any known practice. Although this is indiscriminate, the situation may not be so bad for now, but should it continue, economic doomsday awaits us. Inflation is already biting, dollar is already in short supply, our currency is not an international one and has a perfectly elastic demand, productivity is very low and Foreign Direct Investments and companies are relocating. Yet, instead of a contractionary policy (if needed at all), an apex bank is taking instruction to print money. Yet, it was not proposed for public debates and views but hurriedly done. I doubt whether this was even tabled before the Monetary Policy Committee or not.

The Minister only regretted that one among the same governors who made the request came to raise an alarm about the money printing, just for cheap popularity. As I said, I am a trained economist, not a trained Moral Philosopher to have considered who made the request and who raised an alarm for cheap popularity. So, by all standards, continuous printing of money in this situation will lead our economy to dollarization, as had happened in Zimbabwe. Thank God that Mr. Godwinner spoke out. They will not and should not try it again.

Effects of Inflation

The negative effects of inflation are many; suffice here to say that it had increased the cost, and reduced the standard, of living of Nigerians. We cannot even talk of money illusions now because the incomes of the consumers are not increasing. The welfare losses are too big to contemplate of a once giant of Africa. Moreover, we have a partial coverage economy; where the inadequacies in the labour market are not corrected in the product market. So, the poor, who should deserve some sympathies, are worse hit, because the rich still have some money to spend unjustly and unjustifiably to oppress the poor in the product market. Inflation, thus, is systematically returning us to the B. C. feudal economy of the lords and the serfs.

Possible Solutions

Unfortunately, and without being a "Prophet of Doom", nothing can be done in the lifetime of this administration. We shall only have to manage to ensure that some damage controls are done in order not to worsen the situation. No economist can help revive the economy now. It is too late in the day; the few coming geese are already gone without hatching enough eggs, and even the few hatched have suffered both infant morbidity and mortality to function. However, the good news is that the geese would be back the moment they hear that this administration is gone. The next president would not need to do much, and the economy would bounce back. The leader of the geese (it is a leader-followers hypothesis) abhors nonsense.

Conclusion

It is in our hands. People deserve the leadership they get. If we want illiterates to continue as our philosophers, we should continue to elect leaders with doubtful credentials and expect a system collapse. Arthur Lewis, the founder of Development Economics, likened the sick economy to a patient who needs a physician. It is only if the physician is qualified and good enough that the patient has a chance of survival. However, it can also happen that with the best medical apparatus in the hands of the best physician, the patient still dies".

Then, one reader, perhaps either being inquisitive or still likes Baba Bubu, wrote to ask me for some clarifications and accused me of being biased in favour of the opposition party. I told him that rather, it is my knowledge that always dictates my partisanship in the first place, and not my partisanship dictating my knowledge. Anybody who loves this country cannot sit on the fence, he must take a position. For the avoidance of doubt, below are parts of my reply to him; still in the dream:

"The geese are the Prof. Akamutuse's "Flying Geese". Akamutuse, a Japanese economist, propounded the hypothesis in 1945. They are restless but positive industrial and growth agents. They fly around the world, as dictated by their leader, looking for where to rest and develop the needed capitals they carry on their wings. You are too many ways lucky if the geese are attracted by your endowments, mostly population, even if they soon leave in their restlessness because they do not depart a country with their golden eggs. However, besides population, some deliberate policies must be initiated by the prospective country to attract them.

We have a corruption-development equation. It is only dangerous if the equation is greater than one (>1). There is a minimum level of corruption that must be tolerated in a corrupt society if we would not trade off growth or development. This is especially so when we have a lot of natural disadvantaged destinies, as a country located in the tropic region.

There are usually policies deliberately allowed because development partners are not Father Christmas. Something must be in it for them to come in, and the laymen call everything corruption because they have resemblances that could be likened to identical twins but who have different minds sets. For example, we don't have enough Dollars to stabilize our Naira. The investors who do, would not just bring their Dollars to our country. This is so because there are other countries, which equally need the only world standard currency. We could then carry a tray to them; high interest rate on Dollar higher than it is in their home country, America, or in any of our major competitors. Seeing that their Dollar could yield more profit for them in our country, there could be continuous foreign exchange inflows, even without oil. I had briefly explained the importance of foreign exchange inflows.

Now, another government comes and says why? Why should the Dollar earn more interest here than in their home country, America or in so and so country? The government concludes that some people must be benefiting from it and then, cancel the carrot policy. Then all the Foreign Direct Investors would take their Dollars to those who are ready to do businesses.

Yea, it may be true that some individuals benefited from it, but does a country have to throw away the bathe water and the baby? That was what this administration did and the Naira depreciated as never in our history. The result is imported inflation because we do not produce most of the things we consume, including rice. So, when the President was briefed about the Asian miracle, the critical element of production and others were excluded.

On whether it would have been right for Baba Bubu's government not to fight corruption as he had promised in his campaign or not, mere thinking and ideas will not help us; it must be well articulated policies. Has the corruption gone now? Can corruption ever be speedily zero as they wanted it, especially in a nation ruled by the military for nearly forty years? When the government said they would kill corruption, I laughed, but they soon discovered that if there were no corruption in America and Britain, its meaning would not have been found in the dictionary. This government fought the economic policies of the past administrations, not able to identify Odion from Akhere in a set of identical twin birth with different minds sets, instead of corruption. They realized this too late because they were learners and inexperienced in government, and began to appreciate Dr. Ngoo Dogood and President Jona, but that again was also too late. All the visits of the governors under the President's party to President Jona, which resulted in speculations, real or imagined that they wanted him to be president again under their party, were parts of this belated realization.

What President Jona did was to implicitly forgive past corruptions and tried to use technologies to minimize present and future corruptions in his government. 'Funny' but true; we do not fight corruption so hard - to use Plato's words; "much against their will" - if we would not destroy the gains of the past.

Dear brother, you concluded that my recommendations "have a political undertone". Apostle Paul would have replied this your accusation against me by telling you that if there are such contentions, we have no other custom. If indeed my recommendations are biased, it must be because of the 'limited' knowledge I have about the workings of the economy, especially in an era of speedy globalization, not because of my sympathy with, or affiliation to any political party. No man can do anything about our economy now. We can only do some damage controls.

Nothing, sir, can be done for now. It is already a case of severe disability because Dr. Ngoo Dogood cannot even attract the geese back to our country for now. They simply would not perch here until their conditions are met; mainly that their enemies are out of government. That is their nature. That is why this government has had only two options; tie with the "dragon" in China (only a mad government does that willingly) or continue to borrow. We are almost in economic autarky because we have created uncertainties and skepticisms around ourselves. Maybe I should console you by preaching that God will intervene since we are more Christians, with so many ecclesiastic and their innuendos than the rest of the world. Maybe, that is beyond me.

On whether we cannot live without these development partners or not; yes, if the problem is how we can live between the margins of self-survival, in the face of widening inequalities and poverty. No, if we are interested in growth and development or a radical departure from intergenerational transmission of poverty. Can we do without the Dollar, infrastructures, capital, and manufactured goods, enough of which we can never be able to produce in the lifetime of anybody who is born now? What is our productive base that can make our economy to be self-sustaining? Can we even argue again that Nigeria, not South Africa, is the biggest economy in Africa? Did the argument in some quarters to amend the BRICS as BRI(N)CS to reflect this country not died off since 2015? Therefore, can we say we have scored any goal against our rivals except our own goals with the elections of Baba Bubu in 2015 and 2019?

If we want the dollarization of the country as it was in Zimbabwe, we should continue to print money, to enable us live without the development partners and the rest of the world. If we could grow without them, we would have indeed, been growing without them since 2015. If we have not, then, you should not argue an experiment.

Brother, the patient is already incapacitated in the hands of an unqualified chief physician. You must know more than what you hear or see, because if you do not grow a third ear and a third eye, their propagandas would be your portion.

How did you know that our Central Bank of Nigeria was almost emptied of Dollars, as you have alleged of President Jona's administration? Do we print Dollars? If the Dollars were going empty from the Central Bank of Nigeria, why did the currency instability has to wait for the immediate coming of Baba Bubu before it started? Why did multiple exchange rates have to wait for Baba Bubu? By the way, even at the worst; is it not when you can attract Dollars that you would have to steal? I am telling you that $US86b flew out of the country within six months of Baba Bubu's administration. Was that also because President Jona's men stole Dollars? Like I said, do not allow their propaganda to kill you.

The journey to our bad economy started with the military and was almost completed by the military. However, in the new democracy, Baba Obasara and President Jona, and of course, briefly President Yar'dua of blessed memory had to ensure a resuscitation first and then, growth before we could start talking of development. I did not tell you that they did but that we were on the path to growing like the China and Singapore you mentioned. Consistent growth and foreign exchange accumulation through flagged economic programmes and items took China three consistent decades before the country was noticed. There is no hurry to meet with the lee-way of resources about it at all. The major problem now is that Baba Bubu has taken us way back. Don't even expect him to resign even if he is tired and frustrated in government.

Give me any major leap Baba Bubu had added other than recessions. When illness took him out for six months, the Vice President took us out of the recession, and Baba Bubu's men become annoyed that the Vice President was being praised. That was the end of the Vice President in the government, with a cabal led by the late Chief of Staff nailing him. I mean the Vice President found himself in big trouble for being praised for doing something good.

The story can go on and on. It is simply a lamentation for an otherwise great country, but where illiterates have become the chief philosophers. Even Baba Bubu's Ministers are now lords unto themselves, not bothering reporting to a man who would never understand their simple memos. As far as they can pay homages to the cabals, they are simply okay.

Have you bothered to ask yourself what has happened to the Presidential Media Chat where the President himself used to explain; a programme that was at least, reassuring Nigerians that their president was indeed in charge? Maybe, it is President Jona men's looting of the Dollars that also stopped it. Maybe their looting of the Dollars now makes the "Presidency", instead of the "President" to always speak to us, even on controversial and critical national/economic issues".

"The blames on President Jona's administration is like the proverbial story of an Aanare child (Igberaese, 2018) whose destination was a sure death, but who told his mother to give him palm oil to eat palm nut", I concluded.

He wrote back to me in the same dream to say he doffs his hat for me, but that something must be done. What can be done is simply to wait until we can sweep these clueless people out of government. If he had doffed his hat for me, what would he do for all my teachers and intellectual fathers, who are never to be forgotten but who this country has completely forgotten?

Yet another reader in a WhatsApp group in the dream wrote to warn that people like me should allow the government and the Central Bank to do their jobs.

"Yes, but not so strength because we must engage the authorities", I replied.

"So, what do you know with which you think you can engage them?" He asked.

"What do they have more than me?"

"Answer my question first. What do you have?"

"Alright, I have conquered all available degrees in my profession. I hold a total of four academic degrees, including a doctorate and others certifications. I have enough research outputs to bring to the table. I have won international awards in international conferences, including one held in University of London". Above all, I have been a teacher to the multitude of people whose shoulders this country could rely on, I answered, given his insistence.

"Oga, what they have more than you is corporate experience", he said, perhaps because I did not give detail of my work experience.

"Who told you that? Since I first graduated from the university over twenty years ago, I have never been jobless. The only experience I do not have is embezzlement of public funds and grand corruption.

He did not reply me any longer before I woke up. Maybe that had quenched his anger against me for criticizing bad government policies that may negatively affect him far before me, or he had just known that critics are after all, not, jobless, as he had thought. He had thought that only those in government have corporate experience.

<h1>CHAPTER TEN</h1>

Before the First Century

At the time of setting the foundation for Greek's civilization, Plato (427-247 B.C.), and Aristotle (384 -322 B.C.) who were idealists and realists respectively never agreed on many issues. However, they both agreed that those who should rule the state must be well schooled and pass examinations in Philosophy and Mathematics. That was even in the ancient time; a period before the medieval eras and far before the Anno Domini (A.D.) – the year of the lord. Here we are in the twenty first century, just for hatred, few educated elites, who should know better in our "Common Era" (AD 2015) conspired against an educated president to hand over the country to a semi-literate, who is now the nation's chief philosopher. Yet, the people do not expect a system collapse. Many of those involved have apologized anyway, though their collective apology is the hope that is only good for breakfast but still dangerous for dinner. It is also their collective responsibly to first of all bring us back to where we were in AD 2014 before we can look ahead.

Perhaps, some of them may have had genuine intentions for the country and thought that things would be better if President Jona was out of power, and by all means possible. As the Esan people would say, a woman needs to marry a second husband, before she can tell who between the two men is better. However, the biggest problem now is that the people still believe that The Prof. and men in their mid-eighties should still be the people talking, protesting, and writing. In short, that the great Chinua Achebe of blessed memory should rise from his grave to remind us that "There Was A Country".

Going further, the apologies of the advocates of Baba Bubu have not corrected that widening partial coverage. Their apologies have not corrected the widening inequality Baba Bubu has placed us, in which people once recognized as the happiest people in the world have become the saddest within a few years. Their apologies have not removed us from the wider incidence and higher level of poverty Baba Bubu has bequeathed to us. They have not explained to us why a country once acclaimed as one of the fastest growing economies in the world is now declared the poverty headquarter of the world in just a few years. They have to, since they were, who had told us to hold them responsible for whatever happens if we could remove President Jona from power. They told us to abandon transformation agenda for a change agenda. So, they should let us know how far we have changed and to which direction. If they do not have the answers, I think they should keep quiet forever.

Most of them are engaged in the most sterile occupations, but are the most handsomely rewarded in the country. They have become capitalists without businesses but politics. President Jona on his part had told Nigerians that they would remember him in just two years. Now, every poor person in every nook and cranny of the country is shouting "President Jona", and the shouts started just within a year of his handing over the presidency to Baba Bubu – a period less that he had envisaged. Yet, some of those who promised heaven on earth if and only if President Jona was out of the presidential villa are still shamelessly going round, exonerating themselves from Baba Bubu colossal failure and wishing to be the President of the country, when they are supposed to hide their faces or be in jail. One of them has boldly told Nigerians that Baba Bubu is an epic failure but he has come to correct the evils of his party unto the country. It is simply his turn; only because it is a country of jokers.

The question being asked whenever such an issue as an illiterate leader is raised is whether the President does not have educated cabinet members or not, some of whom are Professors who have done very well in their chosen careers. They do not also remember to ask of what the tail would become when the head is rotten. For example, if a Minister or an aide of the President finds out that his boss is always too dull to understand anything, even what he has severally explained. He would resort to any of the following three options:

1. Quit the job to maintain his integrity, which is hardly an option in Nigeria; largely because of the widening poverty and extended dependency ratios.

2. Stop wasting his time going or talking to the boss and form his side government (a government inside the government), provided he pays his dues to the ruling cabal. Hence, the emergence of a high level lack of synergies among government agencies.

3. Becomes larger than life, does and speaks nonsense in the name of the presidency, if he is a member of the ruling cabal. After all, the President trusts his actions and utterances to be in favour of the cabal, which he ceremonially heads. There would be nobody to caution him since it is not the habit of any member of the cabal to caution another.

Poverty and high dependency ratio would not allow any aide of the President to take the first option of an honourable exit. Even if he may want to, his friends and relatives would not allow him to do so. At least, for their sake, he just has to manage it the way he sees it. After all, there is nowhere it is written in any holy book that he is the person who would repair the country. Is he the only person in the government or was he the person Nigerian people voted for? That is, the buck ends on the President's table. So, those who do not have the minimum education and good health, irrespective of age, for the job are simply not prepared and should never again be allowed to hold the nation to ransom with their inordinate ambitions. The constitutional minimum educational requirement should only be the necessary condition. The sufficient condition; that he must be such who is well educated to be able to raise his head above the water among presidents and comity of nations, should be more emphasized.

The radical and intelligent Catholic cleric from up north, Bishop Matthew Hassan Kukah, herein referred to as

Bishop Matt for the love I have for him, has been telling the Baba Bubu's government the undiluted truth they need to hear about the security and poverty situation in Nigeria. In many of his seasonal greetings to Nigerians, which enlightened Nigerians now look forward to, since the President is incapable of giving them anything to cheer, he has delivered his homely sermons. However, the cabal would not listen to him, not because they do not hear or know that he is incredibly courageous telling the word of truth to the oppressors, but because they have inching ears, to hear only the lies they want to hear. This has in turn, made them truly deaf people. They are very quick to call Bishop Matt names, as if God deemed it fit to consult them before choosing him. I dreamt that it is for the fear of the Catholic Church, not of God, that they have not incarcerated him. Like anything else in the country, it is a paradox that liars are needed by the government more than the truthful people.

It is a bigger paradox that those who are working hard benefit less from the system than the lazy people who hang around the corridors of power, just making noises to please their benefactors, a kind of a concave curve instead of a convex curve, denoting inefficiency; the more inefficient a person is, the more he benefits from the system. It is a paradox that a president of a country would go to a world press to brand his country's hardworking youths lazy and return to the country peacefully to boldly repeat what he had said. Anyway, that had been the views of the country's leaders, who think themselves champions, either because benevolent spirits had smiled on them young, or because they were 'wise' enough to key into the corrupt process with those who carried them on their shoulders. That is why all we have in all sectors of the country are such concave curves.

Like I have said, Nigerian leaders keep quoting J. F. Kennedy out of context; that youths should think of what they would do for the country and not what the country would do for them. Firstly, it was an innocent statement from a sincere president of his country; a country that can indeed, be called a country at all times. It is country where the welfare of the youth is as serious as the air the President breaths in and out. It is a country where the President would do whatever it takes to ensure that no citizen is hungry, naked or homeless. Secondly, when he made that statement, he knew that what America would do for her youths were never in contention. The youths did not have to be the children of the President or of a tiny clique of elites before they could have the three basic necessities of life; food, clothes and shelter. They would get jobs whenever they were ready for the labour market, and in the events of no jobs, the President would be just enough to pay them good unemployment compensations. They would access education and healthcare at minimal cost or no cost. They would not have to watch helplessly, seeing their 'Never Do Well' classmates lording it over them in their later lives, and in all the important Oil and Multi-National Companies, while they were told to go to the farms with outdated implements, simply because their fathers were 'Mr. Nobody' or ordinary Americans. They were not left alone in the wilderness to be self-scavengers where the survival of the fittest would be the rule of the game. They would so get the best things in their lives that how best to enjoy their youthfulness without wasting the assets in them for their coming generations would be their only problem; what J. F. Kennedy was cautioning them about.

Some American youths would not watch helplessly, seeing their counterparts from a section of the same country being spoon fed from the resources from their part of the country, while they were being forced to peace as much against their wills. As big and diverse as America has ever been, her youths would not grow up to meet the offensive statement that some people were born to rule while those from the other parts whose resources are the skeletal core of the country were born to be slaves in their country. They would not wake up to watch criminals and terrorists from the far north of the country being rehabilitated and enlisted in the country's security forces while agitators from the far east are branded terrorists, killed and sent to jails by a man who says he is the President of the country, but who is by default setting, a hater of the easterners. Unfortunately, even elected governor(s) from the east can bravely betray their people to Baba Bubu, provided money or power is involved.

The President is the root and remote cause of the insecurity in Nigeria; every other thing is merely immediate. Let me explain: He had given up the hope of becoming the President after several rejections before Senator Bola Tinubu, herein referred to as Chief Tonobu for the love I have for him, went to resurrect his dead ambition. Believing that he had no more chance of ruling the country, Baba Bubu had concluded that the country should be rendered ungovernable and be burnt down. The only thing he thought of doing was to gather, incite and empower the deliberate army of his impoverished ethnic youths from all over West Africa into crimes and terrorisms against his country, capitalizing on the countries religious and cultural diversities.

Chief Tonobu knew him so well, but his many ambitions pushed him into delivering the great nation to the enemies. Did the terrorists themselves not once name Baba Bubu as their only trustee in any chance of negotiation with the government? Why then should the people be surprised that such a man, who though took an oath to act in the best interest of his country as the President, would be giving such ambassadorial receptions to terrorists and rewarding them with the most sacred jobs in the land? Then, some people are still asking why the widespread rebellions, criminalities and jailbreaks across the country. They ask as if it is written in the old testament of any holy book that God has ordained that a time would come in the land of Nigeria, a country located in the western part of Africa, when mere agitators would be jailed while terrorists would be honoured. Do they not know that injustice breeds its crimes? Injustice, wherever found, is a mother of many crimes. Have they not heard how it has been said that "it is criminal to be law abiding in a city of lawlessness?" Here is a president who had condemned the efforts of his predecessors in fighting terrorism, calling it a fight against the north and crime against humanity. So, it was clear from the beginning that Baba Bubu will never fight terrorists and the rampaging criminal herdsmen and bandits, because he is very sympathetic with their course. It was also clear that he will never fight poverty, because he is not sympathetic with the poor. Nigerians have a president who is anti-poor, instead of being anti-poverty.

The worst of all is that the President does not pretend about his tribal principles and is not bothered about the insecurity in the country. His men know he does not, because as long as the people have refused to forfeit their lands for his tiny tribal Fulani men, to whom he had made ineffable promises of the country's lands, the consequence has to be terrible for the country men. His men also know that for the money from the common patrimony, funding his frequent interval resuscitations in a London hospital, he would have long been in a state worse than being dead. They needless talk to him about anything since his mental disability is now measured almost beyond the Instrumental Activities of Daily Living (IADL), as he could barely recognize anybody without the London doctor's interventions at intervals. However, any cherished news about his tiny tribe, cows and the terrorists are always enough to partially reactivate his brain.

Hence, the only job his party men now have is to unconvincingly defend him before the Nigerian public, even as they are not convinced about him. They have to continuously do so, and against the interests of their people, against their conscience, till his regime is close to an end or is completely over. This is because for now, it is still in him they have access to the country's purse. They are quick to remind Nigerians that the President inherited insecurity in the land, and would even go further to slur the sensibility of the people that he has improved on what he met on the ground.

Once upon a time, one of them, Sen. Smart Adeyemi, herein referred to as Smarto for the love I have for him, summoned up the courage to tell the country and his party men the truth of how the country had been overwhelmed with insecurity. He was nearly crucified by his fellow Senators of the same party on the floor of the Senate.

Smarto had cried out, berating the government for the insecurity situation in the country. He did not insult the President but advocated that the country should put ego aside and seek external help. Another Senator, the wife of Chief Tonobu, called him a wolf in sheep clothing; for dare to have spoken on national issues; against the well-known poor performance of the President. She queried Smarto; whether he was of the major opposition party or not. We saw some Fulani Senators gesticulating and declaring Smarto disgruntled, disgusted, and a disappointment.

For those who do not know, Smarto was brought about by the cabal to displace the flamboyant but avant-garde and activist Senator, Dino Malaye, herein referred to as Dino Meme for the love I have for him. Dino Meme was a sitting Senator who was a bone in the neck of Baba Bubu, for his abysmal performances in government. Hence, Smarto had tried to maintain some modesty all the while. It soon came to a time, a critical period in the lives of the people, when "every onlooker was either a traitor or a coward". Smarto, in his characteristics manner could not simply remain an onlooker. However, with the bashing he got from his party men, it is doubtful whether he would ever cough in the red chamber of the National Assembly again or not.

However, I disagreed with aspect of Smarto's very vibrant speech on the floor of the Senate on that fateful day. Smarto claimed to have spoken on behalf of the man in the street; the hustlers and the poor, but in the context of his speech, he did not. He spoke more on behalf of the affluent. The insecurity targeted by him was kidnapping for ransom, banditry, and none of the insecurities of poverty, unemployment, and inequality in which the country should also remove pride and seek external help. Smarto did not speak for the man in the street because the kidnappers have also come to understand that the man in the street does not have the kind of money they are looking for. This is why they have graduated to banditry, targeting the government and the rich. The bandits mainly target the high profile schools where the children of such rich men as Smarto himself attend, if they are in schools in Nigeria, and not the defenseless public schools for the poor children, even without common fence walls. This has become so because as strategic criminals, the bandits too have come to understand that until an issue affects the rich in the country, it does not call for public concerns. They know that should they continue to kidnap poor children and the man in the street, nobody would listen to them, let alone negotiate and be prepared to pay big money for ransom; for they too, are tired of the high risk venture with peanuts rewards. Smarto did not speak for the man in the street because the man in the street does not travel from the airports where the report he reacted to, said the bandits were targeting.

If he were to speak for the man in the street, he would have remembered that poverty, unemployment, and inequality are the major causes of all insecurities. He would have, in his vibrancy, not recognized merely the symptoms of a disease without the cure. He would have remembered to ask the government to do something about the economy, because the 2004 combined external force of Saddam Hussein and George Bush could never stop insecurity in the country under Baba Bubu's watch that has become the third worse country in the world to live in. Smarto could not have spoken for the man in the street because it had been a long time he left the street, if he was ever there. He no longer know the shape and colour of the street.

Before Baba Bubu instigated the killings in the land, it was just with the ears the people from the vast rural areas of the country heard of crimes like kidnapping, banditry (in schools), raping, and outright slaughtering and massacre of innocent farmers and a whole village. Many generations only read about them in the school as readers and watched such news on television stations as they had happened in other places. These are now mostly perpetuated by his tiny tribal herdsmen from the far north or those of them who immigrated into the country from other neighbouring countries in which they are found – they are not all aborigines of Nigeria. If he were the only person from that tribe who had been privileged to be the President in the country, the story would have been different. It would have made Nigerians be thinking that such were the agenda of all leaders from that tribe. If he were the only adherent of his religion to have become the President of the country, Nigerians would have thought otherwise about that religion. Again, President Yar'dua of blessed memory was a president in the country, though briefly, but long enough for the Fulani herdsmen to have gone on the rampage, simply because their brother was the President. Although I am not of the Islamic faith and do not often read the Quran, I have associates and mentors, including Prof. Hassan Ebhozele Oaikhenan, herein referred to as Prof. Gentle because of the love I have for him, who are Muslims; enough for me to know that Prophet Mohammed was y very peaceful and preached brotherliness, love, and harmony among people of the different religions.

CHAPTER ELEVEN

Such a Bigot

If Baba Bubu were the first president whose tribal men could commit sins against God and humanity, Nigerians would have believed that the constitution permits the President's tribal men to engage in free for all atrocities. President Jona's tribal men threw bombs in the capital city, he got them arrested and served them justice accordingly, because a criminal is a criminal. Up till now, they are still in prisons while those of Baba Bubu's tribe have been released and honoured at the expense of the country's peaceful majority. He ensures his tribal men occupy all the sensitive positions in the country in preparation for the war they had envisaged. For a tribe that is not the first to enter into a country (Ijaw is) and are not known to be one of the most educated (Yoruba is), just imagine their headship of sensitive agencies in the country:

National Petroleum Corporation - Fulani

Federal Inland Revenue Service - Fulani
Custom Service - Fulani
Ports Authority- Fulani
Ministry of Defence - Fulani
Ministry of Finance - Fulani
Ministry of Education - Fulani
Ministry of Justices and Attorney General of the Federation
- Fulani
Ministry of Agriculture - Fulani
Ministry of Aviation - Fulani
Ministry of Communication - Fulani
Ministry of Petroleum - Fulani
Ministry of Water Resources - Fulani
Ministry of Humanitarian Affairs - Fulani
Federal Road Maintenance Agency – Fulani
The Army (Chief of Army Staff) – Fulani
The Police (Inspector General of Police) – Fulani
National Security (National Security Adviser) - Fulani
National Youth Service Corps - Fulani
Television Authority - Fulani
Federal Airport Authority - Fulani
Economic and Financial Crime Commission - Fulani
Independent Corruption Practices Commission - Fulani
NFIU – Fulani; and a host of others.

It is still running and as he winds up, a Fulani man must replace any appointee who is unfortunate to be sacked. The President does such things with reckless abandon. The President is such nepotistic. The President is such a bigot. This is very shameful.

Nigerians have never heard of any news from the Ministry of Commerce and Industry, if it still exists, let alone growing the manufacturing sector. The only thing manufacturing means to the President is the number of new calves that have been birthed by the cows of all the herdsmen in the country. Should any misfortune happens to one cow, the herdsmen have the implicit authority of the President to invade the community in which the cow dies and teach the habitants some bitter lessons their generations would never forget. They have the authority to kill and slaughter not less than five persons in place of one cow that died "unjustly". Cows are more valuable to them than humans because in their views, the direct and indirect costs of growing one cow are higher than the costs of growing five human beings. That is simply what the herdsmen were brought up to understand; at least, before they started realizing that Baba Bubu and companies have been using them. They too, now want to live like their elite Fulani men, resulting in kidnapping and banditry for big money.

They have so resorted because they know that their benefactors have failed them. They have merely been pushed into a war for their elites to gain powers while they mooch from bush to bush. They have come to realize that they should forget about whatever they cannot get now that their chief sponsor is the President because it would be difficult for even another Fulani man to so back them up in their ills. They have watched the Rural Grazing Areas Bill and all the other land conquest bills failed. They, too, have begun to doubt their existence within the next few years when the President must have left office; for not even the non-Fulani Hausa would love them any longer. Yet, they would not call for the President's head. They would make big money now that their chief sponsor is still in charge so that when he leaves office with nobody to protect them, they too would quietly quit their crimes and have enough to fund their life styles. That was their interest in President Jona becoming the President again; a meek man who can easily forgive their past and be focused on the future. They do not trust that others would not bring them to book.

Talking about the non-Fulani Hausa, the story was popularly told of a woman in the south who went to hire some manual labourers. They were all northern chaps struggling for survivals but unfortunately wrongly branded criminals because of the new impression caused by Baba Bubu. To her surprise, one of them raised an alarm that a particular one was a Fulani. They all insisted that he was dangerous in their midst and unless he was out of the vehicle, the rest of them would no longer follow her to her farm. Of course, the woman had no option than to discharge the poor Fulani boy, who also wanted to work hard for a living. That is the much the country has been polarized. That is the much we have been made to be suspicious of, and hate ourselves. It may just be the shadow of things to come; what the President had succeeded in bestowing to his people.

Back to why the herdsmen value the lives of cows more than the lives of humans. All it takes the poor Fulani man to grow a child is simply to cohabitate with, and impregnate a woman or even four at a time. When the child is born, he becomes a street beggar who would survive anyhow. If he does not survive, they would simply summarize his death with some religious invocations, such as "Allah brings, Allah takes". So, even in the latest fight they have been incited to initiate against the country, they have been killed in it more than any singular ethnic group, because a minority can never overwhelm the majority, no matter how much they may try. Yet, they do not care since it is simply

Allah who takes away any of them who dies in the battle. They were brought up to have regards and values for only the lives of their elites and children, who deliberately keep them uneducated and poor for dirty uses. They were taught to always say, for example, "May Allah bless Baba Bubu and his family", not them and their families, after they must have been given some plates of local rice to eat and a cup of local milk to drink by their elites. They were made to believe that Allah has a purpose for creating them poor and their elites rich. They were made to accept the little portion of the earth they were given by men. They did not believe that they were part of the people God told to go and prosper in health and in wealth; Allah only gave them all the lands as their inheritance even if they have to remain in poverty and in squalor.

However, the "exciting times" have come when they have begun to realize that it was in the same way one spermatozoon fertilized one ovum to become any of Baba Bubu's children, that one spermatozoon from each of their fathers also fertilized one ovum to become each of them. This was one of the reasons the northern elites did not appreciate President Jana, who was doing what they did not want; building mega schools to integrate the "almagiri" – street children - into the formal education system, and by implication, attempted to make them wise. As far as Baba Bubu and his clique were concerned, that was the last disservice to humanity President Jona would be allowed to do against the north. Who sent him to destroy their cherished age long culture? They teach that such children are stronger and better cultured in the society. Again I say; God in His throne would be the only judge of this inhumanity, since the children of the elites in that part of the country are never among these children who should be brought up strong in this manner.

Perhaps it seems a joke when it is postulated that President Jona was engaged in a project that the northern elites did not want. One way to validate the hypothesis that they did not like it when President Jona engaged in the "almagiri" integration project is simply to observe that Baba Bubu had long abandoned that project. In short, he has never thought of it since he took office. No one governor, emir, or any of the elites in the north has ever drawn the President's attention to the need to continue the project and take these children out of the street. The only improvement the President has made to the lives of these children is to allow agents freely load them in trucks like goods and transport them to the south, where they could at least, live in better streets and more friendly environments. It is only hoped that they would survival and return home in years. If they do not, "Allah brings, Allah takes".

As busy as the President should be, he wants to know how many new calves have been delivered of all the cows in the country, but he does not want to know how many new industries have been established. It is by his authority that his Fulani legislators are pushing for a bill to establish the Livestock Commission – to be counting and taking records of cows – while smaller countries in Africa are linking all their schools to the internet and preparing visits to the moon. The President wants the Livestock Commission to be counting cows, in a country where the National Population Commission established to count human beings is grossly underfunded.

The President's aides know all the departments and units in the Nigeria National Petroleum Corporation and the

Central Bank of Nigeria, where over eighty percent of the country's money is being generated and manufactured respectively, but they do not know one department of the National Office of Statistics and anything about any Chamber of Commerce and Industry. They do not want to hear from the country's Manufacturers' Association and the President does not know that any such thing as Chamber of Commerce and Industry or Manufacturers' Association exists. The last time the journalists bothered to ask him questions about his plans for manufacturing and industry, his aide interrupted and shifted blame to the fall of oil price in the global market. He regretted that the President did not know why the most important source of foreign exchange earnings to the country should always fall so drastically anytime he was the leader of the country, even though the price was very high during the reign of his immediate predecessor. The answer is very simple. It is a natural order; for the holy book says, when the righteous are in power, the people rejoice, but when the wicked are in power, the people mourn. God has designed it in a way that things will simply not work out to validate the wicked, no matter the propaganda. That also perhaps, means the people deserve what they get whenever they vote a wicked man to power, after all the warnings. Hence, the country is being governed by people with absolute lack of conscience.

CHAPTER TWELVE

This Love for Cows

Those President's cabinet members who still bother to talk to him or wants to brief him on anything would simply develop love for cows, and have his ears. They would first of all tell him how many new calves were born or 'manufactured' in his ranch if they have any access to the ranch. Otherwise, any good breaking news about cows in the country would do to make him smile and be happy. The story was viral on how he demanded the assurance from one of his Ministers from the south who wanted to buy some cows from his ranch. The assurance was that the cows would be killed with all their dignities intact. He stressed that they were what Allah had given to him to cater for, from their birth to death. When the Minister could not understand the dignity of a cow at death and could not give him sufficient guarantee, maybe of employing an anesthesiologist to prevent cows from feeling pains in the process, the President refused to do business with the Minister, who was only in it for the eyes service anyway. That is why the only thing the President knows to do with his iPad set is to monitor his ranch. In short, the President was quoted to have used the words "rest the cow", not "kill the cows" because it would not be dignified for a cow to be killed. This love for cows has also made the quantity and quality of weapon available to the police to control cattle rustling are superior to those to control arm robbery. The most intelligent or brave police and army officers are now deployed to control cattle rustling, not kidnapping and banditry.

Yet, his idea of ranching in the country is only worth it if and only if it would ensure that his minority tribe takes over the ancestral lands of other natives, in their expansionists agenda. Knowing the President's body language and what he stands for, his aides had to warn the people, especially the Benue people, on public television stations to choose between their lands or being killed by the rampaging Fulani herdsmen. This means that the only solution to the reckless killings of the Benue people by the herdsmen was for them to surrender their lands. The herdsmen themselves have come to understand that they have a patron in the President. He had gathered his aggrieved kinsmen from their different countries in Africa and incited them to a "go and occupy or kill" rebellion against his country. Now, that he has become the President by the political dexterity of Chief Tonobu, a man who should have known him better, and who indeed knew him better but for his hungriness for power, the herdsmen did not need to wait for his nod to go killing, because the accord had already been long signed.

No sooner had the President taken over than his kinsmen in the country started to blow the whistle to anywhere they were found in Africa; that the modern author of their radical land conquests agenda was at last victorious. That meant that the country was their next port of call; to find a rescue for their nomadic destinies. Since such lifestyle is often associated with poverty and grime, they had no options other than to take to harmful aggressions. After all, what is it about life for such a people made to dwell in poverty for his elite to dwell in affluence? Instead of the President to see this nomadic destiny of his people as an abnormality and finding ways by the singular opportunity he has gotten as the President, to genuinely rescue them from it once and for all, he decided to send them on a war they can never win. So far so good, they have not succeeded despite being allowed to freely go about with AK-47 rifles, tied under the bellies of cows and cattle.

Although they have taken over the army and the police, just to give themselves tactical supports in the war, they have still been worse off. Yet, the President's and their elites' children are not among those in the warfronts. His children attend the best schools in Europe and America, preparing to come back and lord it over their people like their father did. He prefers such a widening gap to closing the poverty gap. He likes it better when his own Fulani people are unable to break out of their intergenerational transmission of poverty. Why should the rest of us be angry when as the President, Baba Bubu has preferred for his own people, the obsolete ideology of wars for land conquest to the modern ideology of maximum welfare? Yes, wars about land is obsolete because he who owns even a 100ft by 100ft of land owns it to the sky and with money, he could build a skyscraper that would accommodate a his tribe.

Now, Nigerians have so far overwhelmed them that they fear their fates whenever their chief patron is out of power. The President's mute about their activities are the validations of the hypothesis that the police and security agencies are with them. Indeed, the whole of the north is now suffering in silence, because they could not now be seen casting aspersions on one of their own, who they have earnestly asked Allah for.

Chief Tonobu is indeed a political master strategist, no doubt (especially when he was young with all the good health and strength). However, he got it wrong by thinking that Baba Bubu and his cabal would reward him. As a man who does a lot of planning, he knew that there was no way his Yoruba race could have become the President as at the time of the planned onslaught against President Jona. Therefore, he went to resuscitate a dead ambition for a North and South-West alliance. He had believed strongly that he would easily take over as the President by the reciprocal benevolence of his beneficiary, at the end of his tenure, going by the reward system. Things started falling apart the moment the President was sworn in. Right from the public venue of the oath taking, he declared, to let Chief Tonobu know that if there was any semblance of an accord between them, it was all a playing along game he was only compelled to accept by his cabals, if he would become the President of the country. Therefore, he would not do Chief Tonobu's bidding, neither was he for Chief Tonobu. It was not a statement for the nation as widely perceived but a message to Chief Tonobu that he should stay clear of the corridor of power. It is a pity that Chief Tonobu and his people would never understand how the President's Fulani tribe believes that they could always use the intelligence of the south western majority tribe against the south. If the President's people are not wise and educated, or poor, it is not in politics; it is not when political power is involved. They do not need to solve any calculus or speak any foreign language to prognosticate and fix any political brouhaha to their advantage. They understand the meaning of political power and know the language it understands. They know how to prepare the medicine for the educated south western people of the country.

Chief Tonobu should have seen the handwriting on the wall when he was not accepted as the running mate to Baba Bubu, as he had envisaged of his first and immediate planned ambition. He had surrendered a political party he had so much laboured to build and envied for its domination of the south-west, in the name of a coalition. It only happened that they found an excuse in Muslim–Muslim ticket, as if it had not happened before in the country, with the election adjudged as the freest and fairest in the country's history – so they said because I was still too young to dream by that time. Without justifying such primitive ticket in a polarized country in this era, they however only saw it as an excuse for a too strong a character to be the vice to a weaker candidate as the President. Muslim-Muslim ticket would have been more lucrative and less controversial at that time because:

1. The presidential candidate was a Northern Muslim who the north saw as their darling.

2.   Baba Bubu had not been the President to have had the chance to so polarize Nigeria along the sides of tribe and religion. Although these things were parts of the country's problems, they were not as disdained as they are nowadays; after Baba Bubu's damage to the country.

So, they only feared that Chief Tonobu would overshadow the President; that they would be unable to control him. The multidimensional appointments of his estranged godson, Babatunde Fashola, a Senior Advocate of Nigeria, herein referred to as Bab Fash for the love I have for him; a former decent governor of his state, was another meant to cut the chief to size. To empower the else governor to take over the leadership of his state and south west from Chief Tonobu, he was overloaded with multiple "Grade A" ministerial functions. The workloads overwhelmed him, and within two years, Bab Fash grew the grey hairs he did not grow in eight years as the governor of the biggest state in the country. It was either the else governor was too decent to be interested in picking any dirty fight with Chief Tonobu or as an intelligent man, he foresaw that Chief Tonobu's influence would be too much for him to wrestle with. In which case, he has so far disappointed his federal benefactors, even though he too has his professional integrity and personality that must be respected as an asset to the government, even by his estranged godfather.

If Chief Tonobu continues to pursue his presidential ambition – of course, he will, because he has characters that never say 'die' – his adversaries in the north would continue to encourage him so that he would invest part of his wealth in that part of the country. They would only tell him their minds when it is too late. They have already raised his godsons, Prof, Yemi Osinbajo, herein referred to, as his boss has already called him, Prof. Osinbade for the love I have for him, against him. There is nobody who would be told that he has a chance of becoming the President of the country that would throw it away because of Chief Tonobu. Even his wife would not, let alone the average Nigeria politician, who is only loyal to himself. Chief Tonobu would fight dirty with everything at sight to get what he wants because his heart is injured by Baba Babu's betrayal; nobody can stand on his way except the northerners.

Although illness and the same circumstance of medical tourism, which Nigerians have criticized a lot once reunited Chief Tonobu and Baba Bubu in London, snapping pictures together for Nigerians to know that they were not yet dead, it did not mean that Baba Bubu is with him. He is not yet the President and old age related illnesses have started taking him to a London Hospital. What if the unprecedented duties of the President are added to his present loads? Why is it that we do not even tell ourselves the truth? Has he not achieved enough to be proud of himself and his people, and to be grateful to God without being the President?

However, Nigeria is another country entirely; the sicker the politicians are the more they want to be the President (and the more they want to hold political offices) or actually become one. So that they can use public funds to merely extend their lives without the needed productivities. In the London meeting of Baba Bubu and Chief Tonobu, It became a two man "Association of Sick President and Sick Ambitious President" (ASPSAP) meeting in London hospital at a time resident doctors in their home country were on strike for lack of welfare and entitlements. It is only in Nigeria such a thing can exist and the men would still get red carpet reception when they return into the country – peaceful people! Government functionaries and traditional rulers would line up to welcome them, and further humiliate their poor citizens who have no access to healthcare in the country they lead. Cultural dances closed to the airport and in the palaces would be boldly shown on national television stations welcoming them back from superfluous sickness leaves without fear or shame, because oppression and corruption now thrive with reckless abandon. Poor citizens would be registered to sing and dance for them! Should the poor citizens not even be happy that they were given the exceptional privilege to see how the airport and their prominent citizens look like? They should be delightful, idyllic and have the memories of seeing Baba Bubu and the airport at close range to relish.

Yes. I have merely followed Baba Bubu on the name the Vice President; Prof Osinbade is given here. This is because it was Baba Bubu who first gave him that name, and in the words of Baba Bubu, in the "All Progressive Confident Party", instead of the "All Progressive Congress". This was shamefully in an interview with a foreign journalist during their presidential campaign.

The foreign journalist had remarked, wondering how overcast the person chosen to be the President of the most populous country in Africa was, before he actually became one. I dreamt that the President did love his vice till his illness that kept him in London for several months, wasting resources and increasing the country's Disability Adjusted Life Years (DALYs), Costs of Illness (CoI), and overall Burden of Disease (BoD). He had insisted that Prof. Osinbade act as the President despite all odds from members of his cabal. Prof. Osinbade took the job head on. Following the antecedence laid down by President Yar'dua of blessed memory, he parley with the Niger-Delta militants and brought Nigeria out of the recession, which Baba Bubu had put her. Hardly did he know that he was violating "Law 1" of the Robert Greene's "The 48 Laws of Power", outshining his master.

The nation was elated and started showering praises on him, and the information Baba Bubu continued to receive about this state of affairs in his sickbed was disheartening. He heard that Nigerians, especially those from the south were praising Prof. Osinbade at his expense, and this increased his illness. As usual about the religious and ethnic brainwashing in the country, acknowledging Prof. Osinbade for evidently doing well became a matter for division between the north and the south, and between the Muslims and the Christians. It also meant to the cabal that he was playing smart and wanted the President dead so that he would be sworn in as the President. The mere fact that he spoke better in English to analyze and address the country's problems without reading prepared speeches all the time was a problem between the north and the south, and between the Muslims and the Christians.

Since the President did not die; at least (it was rumored he did, and even the most educated person in the country did not know what to believe any longer because Nigeria is a country where a horse could fly), still breathing, the cabal went on an emergency meeting and the singular agendum was Prof. Osinbade. They came out with a singular outcome to keep Prof. Osinbade in check, but not without brainwashing the President against him, which they succeeded in doing. A lot of terrible things and humiliations, which are outside the scope of my dream narration, happened to Prof. Osinbade; as a person and as the Vice President, but as I have said before, quitting is not an option in Nigeria. Moreover in his case, if he had dared to quit, Chief Tonobu and his cohort would have taken advantage; for they had not been happy with him, since envy had set in that he only occupied the master's seat and without enough loyalty to him or enough patronage for them overtime. They were also afraid of the praises Nigerians showered on him when he acted. That meant to them that he was closer to the presidency than Chief Tonobu and if things continued that way, he might just be chosen as Baba Bubu's successor at the expense of Chief Tonobu.

However, something still went for him that elicited public likeness for him despite his emasculation by the cabal. That is, he remained a Professor worth his salt; one in its true sense of the word. It was the only thing he had to be superior to the cabal and they could not immediately do anything about that. That was why at the death of the head of the cabal; the infamous Chief of Staff to the President, they have to bring in a higher ranking Professor than Prof. Osinbade. They had thought of a man to whom Prof. Osinbade must always doff his hat according to the respected tradition in academics, as a replacement for the late Chief of Staff. In their views, that would intimidate not just Prof. Osinbade but also the South-West, if they had thought that Professors were only found in their zone. Moreover, that would at least, convince the world that it was not for the lack of Professors among them that they had presented a near illiterate as the President. It would also finally crush the Vice President if he sees a more experienced and older Professor in the Federal Executive Council.

It only happened that as an old Professor of repute, the new Chief of Staff became not interested in the arrogance show off of power and oppressions like his predecessor. He had told the cabal that being a man who had represented the country at the global stage and considering his age, he wanted to rest as a private citizen. They begged him to remove the shame from them, believing that the moment he accepts, they would gradually implant the ideas of the cabal in him. It is not that the north does not have enough Professors. They needed a particular one that could intimidate the South-West, one that would have no reason to respect Prof. Osinbade, and if possible, one whose credentials and antecedents are capable of intimidating Prof. Osinbade. Those are the kinds of narrow minded thoughts of the self-serving cabal ruling the country, since the President does not know his left from his right. The new Chief of Staff started disappointing the cabal when he had announced to the whole country as soon as he took over the office, that he is only responsible to the President. That is, he would not be a member of any cabal; for which he has so far and so good, disappointed them.

Nevertheless, No one cares about their shows of power. Unlike during President Jona's administration, there are more than enough substantial problems now surrounding daily survivals of the citizens than to mind any person who is enveloped in power. There are insecurity and hunger, which have brought Nigeria down to becoming the second country in the whole world with food scarcity, only next to Syria, and the poverty capital of the world. These basic needs problems are enough daily battle to downplayed the minds of many Nigerians from their self-actualization needs in which they had enthusiastically picked interests, let alone interest in what the cabals think of themselves. Nigeria is now brought down to the level of the President; of course, a country can only be as good as its leader. Nigerians no longer care about what happens to their darling Super Eagle football team, nor do they care any longer about who is the national football coach who used to be more popular than the governor of any state. They care no longer about who is disqualified from the Olympic team or how many medals are won or not won. They no longer care about any Olympic qualification of the age grade football team, which was called the "Dream Team" 1 to whatever number. They no longer care whether it is Ghana or Nigeria that qualifies for any World Cup holding in anywhere. All Nigerians now think about is how they can survive in the jungle-like country and how many days still remaining for Baba Bubu's tenure to end – the question every dick and harry now ask. All the adults now think about is how to first of all repair the country, before thinking of sports. All that the youth now thinks about is how to just leave the country; to anywhere, and Ghana is usually not a bad idea since it is the nearest visa free country for Nigerians. They now think about how to make money by all means, including ritual killings, to rescue their families. However, anybody who dares talk or write would incur the wrath of Baba Bubu's stationed security men to arrest and to intimidate any opposing voice.

Baba Bubu's supporters argue that Nigeria is not the poverty capital of the world. They continue to roll out the Gross National Income or the Per Capita Income data of poor countries and challenging the other people to point out

Nigeria from the first to the tenth position of the poor countries in Africa. Firstly, is it not a big shame that Nigeria is now being compared with countries like Somalia, when in about six years before Baba Bubu, her economy was arguably bigger than that of South Africa? How the country got to this record low level in just six years does not worry them.

Secondly, they do not really understand the difference between poor countries and the poverty of a county. Dudley Seers (1969) was the first to raise the alarm on the mistake of using Per Capita Income to measure development. Seer asked: "what has been happening to unemployment? What has been happening to poverty? What has been happening to inequality?" He wrote that if any of these or all three are not going down, it would be strange to call the result development even if Per capita income doubles. Amatya Sen, the 1998 Nobel Prize winner in economics extended this to include some welfare indexes in the measurement of development. Since then, growth has been differentiated from development with the latter being "Growth plus change", and with the kind of change Baba Bubu has brought to Nigeria, it would now be expedient to qualify the "change" with "positive". For the record, Igberaese (2004) also develops four windows of looking at the poverty of a country, with Nigeria belonging to the Rich-Poor window, where the country is rich but the people are poor.

As I have said, since Nigerians are already accustomed to poverty and squalors, they do not even understand how much they dwell in the vicious cycle of poverty. This, the Igberaese's paper calls the intergenerational transmission of poverty, whereby children inherit poverty from their parents. The author posits that the country needs a radical departure to break out of such an ugly situation. Then, if telling the pointblank truth to the oppressors of Nigerians is my little way of achieving this, it is radical enough.

Let us even leave Seers and Sen out of the Nigeria's case and look at the five most important goals of macroeconomics, namely; economic growth, full employment, price stability, exchange rate stability and balance of payments equilibrium.. In which of them can Baba Bubu's supporters beat their chests to be better than any past governments order than put excuses on the dining tables of Nigerians?

I know that my choice of words of the infamous Chief of Staff seems to be offensive, especially with a culture of respecting the dead, but how did the majority of Nigerians see him? Why should I be held responsible for a fact that was revealed to me in my dreams? He held swell in office as a superman, thinking that the feast would never end, let alone thinking of his death, didn't he? The office of the Chief of Staff, which was supposed to be a Principal Private Secretary to the President was so exalted to be the President, wasn't it? He had the power of sharing and the power of firing anybody from the cabinet and even had the power to determine who got elected or re-elected to any position, hadn't he? He sent old foes to jails and vowed to keep them there, didn't he? He died like the biblical foolish man, didn't he? Above all, Nigerians, including Oshemore, the then National Chairman of the ruling party, with a heartbreaking exercise for his age, celebrated, instead of mourning at his death, didn't they? So, now, you are convinced that I did not coin the word "infamous", aren't you?

When some cliques started lambasting the people for rejoicing over a person's death, I laughed. Once again, when Gen. Abacha died, the people rejoiced? However, when another President from the north, Yar'dua died, the people did not rejoice but resigned to sober reflection, took out time to mourn a good man. No one needed to be passing messages, reminding Nigerians that it was not our culture or in our custom to rejoice at a person's death. It was simply natural not to celebrate but to mourn Yar'dua because the life he lived or how he led the people with the opportunity God had given him was judged by his country men and women he left behind. The people only flay at how his illness was mismanaged by a cabal who wanted to take advantage of his illness and death of the President.

If Baba Bubu was treated in the country he leads and had died in the country, would it have restored the happiness he was elected to increase for Nigerians, but which he has taken away from majority of them? Would enormous resources not have been saved for investments in critical infrastructures? If the answers to these questions are yes, then, he should have returned the happiness that he had stolen from the people!

CHAPTER THIRTEEN

Overall Burden of Disease

We now come to the important health economics issue of how the overall BoD (to fully understand the priority areas for public health intervention) for Nigeria would have been reduced through DALY and CoI (Murray & Lopez, 1996), if the President had maintained his dignity or remained a man of his own words. That is, if he had not gone to the London hospital for treatments upon his disease infection, as he had promised during his campaign and at the worst, make either a direct demand or an indirect demand for death. I shall attempt a very lucid theoretical background on this so that the gains of the country from such demand for death by an ailing president would be very clear; so that you may know that I write not of my own but by inspirations.

We talk of "Mr. Integrity" because Baba Bubu had promised either to fix the Nigerian health sector or die here in Nigeria whenever he is ill. The people cannot forget how much he had criticized Late President Ya'dua for seeking healthcare outside the country. Everyone expected that he would go the way of Dr Nelson Mandela of blessed memory when he fell ill. Dr Mandela did not go to a hospital anywhere other than in his country, South Africa and he died there. Being a former soldier, Baba Bubu was expected to be the practical leader of the army as he had boasted during his campaign. Idriss Deby of Chad Republic did it in his country and died for his belief. Like Mamma Gadaffi of Libya and others, the President would have behaved like those who refused any foreign trip or exile, thereby dying as heroes for their countries.

One fallacy the proponents of Baba Bubu as Mr Integrity have committed over the years is the fallacy of composition; taking a part of him to be the whole of him. They, thus, evaluate his first regime of yesteryears. Even at that, they still committed the fallacy of association by forgetting or mischievously so, that it was his second in command, who was the proponent of, and in charge of the "War Against Indiscipline and that 'war' was the only philosophy of that regime that should have become a legacy.

DALY is a health stop-gap measure, or one of the composite measures in the calculation of BoD, as propounded by Murray and his co-worker in 1996. DALY is calculated by the additions of Years of Life Lost (YLL) to mortality and Years Lived in Disability (YLD), with a weight factor between zero and one, depending on the severity of the disability. That is:

$$DALY = YLL + YLD \qquad (8)$$

Where: YLL is the multiple of the summation of all fatal cases due to healthy outcomes of a specific disease (d_i) and the expected life span of the individual at the age of death (e_i). Hence:

$$YLL = \sum_I d_i \times e_i \qquad (9)$$

YLD is calculated by the multiple of the summation or accumulation of all cases and all health outcomes (n_i) by the duration of illness (t_i) and the disability weight of a specific disease (w_i). Hence:

$$YLD = \sum_I n_i \times t_i \times w_i \qquad (10)$$

So that if we substitute equations (9) and (10) into equation (8), we have:

$$DALY = \sum_I d_i \times e_i + \sum_I n_i \times t_i \times w_i \qquad (11)$$

CoI, as seen in Oostenbrink and his co-workers in 2004, is the accumulated Direct Healthcare Cost (DHC), Direct Non-Healthcare Cost (DNHC), and Indirect Non-Healthcare Cost (INHC). The calculation excludes Indirect Healthcare Cost (IHC), which is the future savings on healthcare cost as a result of premature death. That is, the cost that would have been incurred in direct medical services if the individual were still alive or if he had not died of the specific disease, but still in a state less than full health or suffering from a disability as a result of the specific disease. Ideally, this cost cannot be easily determined.

DHC are costs of general consultations, cost of specialist consultations, costs incurred as a result of hospital attendance (in-patients or out-patients or both), costs of drugs, costs of rehabilitation, and of other disease progressions, and so on, before the restoration of full health. For each healthcare outcome of a specific disease and each medical health service, the DHC related to a specific pathogen is given by the equation:

$$\Sigma \left(\Sigma_i \, m_i \times p_i \times mc_i \right)_1 \qquad (12)$$

Where: m_i is the number of cases requiring healthcare
p_i is the required healthcare service unit per case, and
mc_i is the cost per healthcare service unit.

DNHC is the cost incurred on traveling, additional costs incurred on diapers, medical expenditure on other illnesses different from the specific disease, but discovered during the treatments of the specific disease. Also included are co-payment for drugs and other informal cases, like motivation for a caregiver as a result of disability from the specific disease. For each direct non-healthcare outcome of a specific disease and each non-healthcare service, the DNHC related to a specific pathogen is given by the equation:

$$\Sigma \left(\Sigma_i \, r_j \times q_j \times rc_j \right)_1 \qquad (13)$$

Where: r_j is the number of cases requiring non-healthcare service
q_j is the required non-healthcare service unit per case and;
rc_j is the cost per non-healthcare service unit.

DNHC is however said to be very negligible and relatively small when compared to the other costs, which are usually included in the CoI analysis. For this reason and lack of appropriate data, DNHC is also usually not included in the CoI analysis.

However, I have to contend this exclusion of DNHC in Africa, where there is a huge deficit in infrastructure and a lack of social security. For example, transportation fares are not negligible and in the absence of the government taking responsibility of nursing homes, the relative of the sick needs to pay well if he must have a caregiver. Many African rich people pay huge amounts for flights overseas for medical attention. In the specific case of Baba Bubu, it involved a whole presidential jet and the hiring of expert caregivers, to match his status as the President. These can be accounted for through the source documents upon payments, especially with the Freedom of Information Law.

The other cost to be included is INHC, which is the value of production loss to society as a result of absence from work, whether for a temporary or permanent or long term disability or premature death. It also includes the loss of productivity from sickness leave of individual and that of a third party taking care of the sick individual. This was very obvious for the more than six months the President stayed in a London hospital and for all the frequent medical trips at intervals he continues to make. This is especially so that the Vice President no longer act to fill the vacuum as the cabal had already succeeded in cutting him to size.

INHC can be calculated as follows: For each indirect non-healthcare outcome of a specific disease and each type of sickness leave:

$$\Sigma\ (\Sigma_i\ s_k \times V_k)_l \tag{14}$$

Where: S_k is the number of sickness leave

U_k is the duration of sickness leave and;

V_k is the wage cost per day.

(Partly extracted from Igberaese & Iseghohi, 2017. The burden of disease calculation, cost of illness analysis and demand for death: A theoretical review. *INJODEMAR*. Development and Management Review Group, Federal University of Technology, Owerri; Chicago State University & Tshwane University of Technology, Soshanguve – An African Journal Online and A Society of Africa Journal Editors indexed).

Although the analyses above are mainly of public health policies, we can also take a micro look at them because the individual persons make up the community.

Murray and Oostebrink on DALY and CoI respectively were just products of their western environments, not of Africa. That is why I hold the view that Direct Non-Healthcare Costs are not negligible in Africa, especially in the case of the President, in which the cost of transportations; on presidential jets to and fro London, and those of his caregivers are huge sums, enough for some infrastructural developments in the country. Since such costs are expected to be backed up by source documents, they should be included in the President's CoI analysis. Again, from what was spent, we can estimate the supposed future savings, if the President had demanded death to free resources for his country's development. After all, he would not live forever. Hence, we can ascertain the Indirect Healthcare Costs. Therefore, IHC should be included in the CoI analysis occasioned by the terrible ill health of the President.

For the avoidance of doubt, demand for death was pioneered by us; Igberaese, Ogheneovo, and Iseghohi in 2017, and led by me. We were a small group of Ph.D. students of Economics, specializing in Health Economics in the University of Benin. We extended the Gruenberg's work of 1997 on the "Failure of Success (FoS) Hypothesis". We were worried that Healthy Life Expectancy (HALE), a prolonged life that is accompanied by a similar extension of a healthy life, was never considered in Africa in measuring the life span of a person. Africans merely emphasize Life Expectancy; a prolonged life not accompanied by similar healthy life. That is, longevity does not imply a healthy life for productivity and growth and development of the country.

We saw demand for death as a possible remedy for excessive BoD and CoI. That is, only when disability is already measured beyond the Instrumental Activities of Daily Living – IADL (referring to disabilities affecting a broad range of activities, such as telephone use, shopping, housekeeping, preparation of food, doing laundry, use of various types of transport, handling of drugs, and management of finances). When disability is beyond such measure, it reaches the Activities of Daily Living – ADL (showing the dependence of an individual on other individuals to assist in daily life; such as it was for Baba Bubu in London). It is the most severe case of disability; without being able to be involved in feeding, bathing, and dressing, moving from bed to chair or from one chair to the other, among others by himself. We found that the case of Nigeria is entirely a validation of the failure of success hypothesis. We also found that many have demanded death to end BoDs and CoIs, but that they were not empirically recognized since they were off records.

Demand for death is categorized into direct and indirect: (i) direct demand for death is when the individual with a specific disease eats or injects a poisonous substance into his body system, either by himself or through the assistance of another person, say a physician or non-physician or a clinician. However, the individual can only remain healthy at death if the death is sold to him by an expert physician because vital healthy organs could still be harvested for medical purposes before the death. (ii) indirect demand for death is when the individual with the specific disease deliberately ignores the advice of a medical practitioner against certain foods or drinks that are capable of accelerating the death of that individual. Indirect demand for death can also occur when the individual refuses to take or be administered drugs that could shift his death time forward into the future. It can also occur when the individual oughts for voluntary discharge from the hospital against the advice of a medical practitioner, in the case of in-patient, or refuses to keep doctor's appointments, in the case of out-patient.

I should emphasis again that, which I had said before: Countries should thus never wait for citizens to do the terrible demand for death before investments in health should be made. This is because as important as health market goods are, it is unlike the product market goods that deserve a top position in the individual's scale of preference because their immediate needs are so self-manifest for that individual. For example, hunger would make a family head immediately make foods a top priority. The fear of stress from trekking to work every day will make a man put the constant repairs of his car on top of his budget, even if the car has not completely broken down. However, many people would not think of adding to their health stocks before they are completely broken down. There is not so much awareness and resources to fix bad health that is yet unseen let alone nipping it in the bud. Thus, it is a subordination of individual interests to general interests for any manager of a country to believe that it is the individual's responsibility to take care of his own health needs. Good enough, the partial coverage in the product markets can easily be corrected in the health goods market through population health intervention. This should make public interventions easier in favour of the poor.

If Baba Bubu was a man of honour; a man of his words, he would never have sought medical care abroad because as he had said, elected officers were not different from the electorates. He would have simply lee on the options of indirect demand for death and remained a hero who even at death delivered on his promises. This would have restored the happiness he had promised the people but which he had taken away from them. He would have helped his country by reducing DALY and CoI.

Fortunately, and unfortunately for Nigerians, as Igberaese and co-workers have advocated, demand for death can only be based on self-reported limitations – disabilities. Nobody has the right to negotiate life on behalf of another person no matter how close a relative. Fortunately, because this wicked government would have killed all its sick citizens through a policy of demand for death. Unfortunately, because I dreamt that a greater number of Nigerians would have helped the President in such an abnormal demand (including some of his Ministers) – because the demand for death does not obey the downward slopping demand curve or the law of demand. It is a concave curve like the health production function, denoting inefficiency (since those who are sicker benefit more from the produced health goods and services). We can easily see that the lower the price of death, the higher the demand for life and thus, the lower the demand for death. This is a Robert Giffen type of goods.

I have still not fully answered the question of how the President's demand for death would have benefited the country. From the calculation of DALY = YLL + YLD
When death is demanded at ADL measured disability, DALY will be reduced. The YLD would be reduced and

tend towards zero. DALY will thus be equal to only YLL, simply becomes the number of years of life lost due to mortality. Then, the DALY equation would simply decompose to:

$$DALY = YLL \tag{15}$$

However, Murray and company did not see this, perhaps because in their environment where there are many healthcare models and with functional healthcare systems, healthcare delivery is at its peak, and citizens rarely or never get to ADL measured disability.

Hence, the multiple of the summation of all fatal cases due to healthy outcomes of a specific disease (d_i) and expected life span of the individual at the age of death (e_i).

$$\text{Thus, } DALY = \Sigma_I \, d_i \times e_i \tag{16}$$

This is a big reduction in BoD because the only loss becomes the productivity the individual would have engaged in if he had not died of the specific disease before the age he was normally expected to die. It has removed the entire burden that he and his relatives, including that of his caregiver, would have borne if he had not died, but continued to live in the state of ADL disability; a state worse than being dead. It is a disease that would have still eventually caused him to die before his expected life span anyway.

From the CoI analysis, the demand for death would increase IHC, the future savings on healthcare cost as a result of his premature death. DHC would approach zero, DNHC would also approach zero while INHC would remain constant (not increasing) upon the demand. The analysis would then include IHC because his relatives (in the case of the President, the country) will be able to estimate what they have saved since his death (from what they used to spend during the illness). Then, for each healthcare outcome of a specific disease and each medical health service, $\Sigma\ (\Sigma\ m_i \times p_i \times mc_i)$ would approach zero. For each direct non-healthcare outcome of a specific disease and each non-healthcare service, $\Sigma\ (\Sigma_i\ r_j \times q_j \times rc_j)_l$ would approach zero.

The loss of productivity from sickness leave of individual and that of a third party taking care of the sick individual, $\Sigma\ (\Sigma i\ us_k \times V_k)l$ would remain constant, and in the case of the President, the country would have the opportunity to replace him with a more healthy individual. And IHC, which is the savings from the future cost would approach infinity.

This again is a great gain from demand from death, as the individual's relatives and the society can channel such resources to other productive uses. Oostenbrink and company did not see this. These costs are negligible in their regions because of their responsive governments, which had provided good infrastructures, and functional insurance systems.

Nigerians did not gain these in the case of the President. Yet, he had remained unaware of the citizen's sacrifices to keep him alive and of the happenings in his country, except for cows and his Fulani group.

Chapter Fourteen

And the Problem Continues

The problem continues, as the President has continued to incur all costs; worsening the CoI analysis of Nigeria. This is so because his illness has become terminal since he needs a London hospital to stay alive. In the measurement of the Quality Adjusted Life Years (QUALYs), this is a case worse than being dead. It is worst when the health budgets for the President is not to add value to the country's Gross Domestic Products, but constitute capital freight. When disability comes with a shot down brain, it is hardly noticeable but the effects on relatives and communities are real. In the case of the President, all citizens are his relatives and the country is his community, because the success of every business and endeavour depends largely on government policies, which require a very sound brain. Britain can only continue to treat him on the basis of the

"Out-of-Pocket Model" of healthcare delivery, which is non-existent among her citizens and shamefully the only known model prevailing in his country.

In the Out-of-Pocket Model system, no real organized healthcare system operates. Individuals pay for healthcare from their pockets, while doctors charge according to their discretions. This is what operates in Nigeria. So, many people could live a whole life without access to doctors but village healers using brewed herbs, with their efficacies subjects of probabilities. The rules is that the rich access healthcare while the poor remain sick, or die of even minor diseases, if they cannot pay to live long. What this means is that while the poor with good healthy expectancy for high productivity end up with short life expectancy, the rich with bad healthy expectancy end up with long life expectancy. Pregnant women who are afraid of high doctors' bills manage their pregnancies with Traditional Birth Attendance (TBA) or with quack doctors. Some die from preventable diseases. The most frequent example of how the Out-of-Pocket model of healthcare affects maternal cases is when the poor women who are afraid of the hospital bills from cesarean sections decide to opt for vagina deliveries against doctors' advice. As rich as Nigeria is, being the sixth biggest crude oil producing country in the world, she is ironically one of the countries that cannot provide affordable healthcare for at least, her pregnant women, thereby sentencing them to death in the process of bringing other human beings to this world. What a big shame!

However, I have recently observed, and in collaboration with other researchers, writing of an emerging healthcare model in the country. Although it is a little bit improvements of the Out-of-Pocket model, it is not of consciously directed efforts of the government. It is only necessitated by the managements of public hospitals to savage an abandoned health sector. The purpose of the writing is to provoke researches and grants for a better and sustainable health model in our country but only in a country that has caring leaders. For convenience, we can call it the "Case Note Model" of healthcare delivery, even though it is just an unrecognized healthcare practice.

In the "Case Note Model", patients, especially those on emergencies are not abandoned to die in hospitals because they have no money to pay from their pockets. Unlike with the Out-of-Pocket model, treatments of such patients commence immediately with the little resources available to the hospital without yet asking for payments, except their relatives can afford to do such immediate payments. All the costs of treatments are recorded in the case notes of the patient, while treatments continue to the stage where the illnesses are no longer life threatening. The objective of the "Case Note Model" is to save the patients from the life threatening condition, after which their relatives are expected to look for money for further treatments. Since the hospitals do not get additional supports from the government, it is limited to saving the life of the emergency patient and not to go further in his treatments or to make him fully recover. There are cases when the patients would be stabilized enough to give his relatives a clue on how payments for their treatments can be made. Moreover, the relatives, being relatively sure that the patients' survival rates are high, are encouraged to help out with the costs of treatments till the patients are discharged from the hospitals.

Most times, the hospitals are not able to continue treatments beyond a defined stage since the little resources available would be rationed among many poor patients in this manner. Moreover, there are still some patients who die because of the lack of funds to continue treatments, which become losses to the hospitals. The extent to which these hospitals can continue to treat these many poor patients and incurring losses is very doubtful. However, the BODs still continues even after the patients have fully recovered from the illnesses or died. This is because most families have to work extra hard for a long time to pay back what they had borrowed to offset the direct costs of the illnesses. In some cases, the hospitals would be compelled to give reasonable discounts, especially if the patients are so poor or do not survive.

I believe that even with the limitations, it is an innovation better than the Out-of-Pocket model deserving of good report since upon arrival at the hospitals, the patients are not abandoned to die for their lack of resources for treatments. Moreover, it has encouraged more access of the poor population to doctors and enhanced utilizations of hospital resources. Just which government would come in at this stage for some improvements on this indigenous model? That is not at all in Baba Bubu's regime. He and his cabal are not thinking in that direction.

In what is another strand of it", is its use for maternal cases. The hospitals ensure that pregnant women are attended to and are delivered of their babies safely, irrespective of their insurance or income status, which are predominantly low among the poor women. The new babies are well taken care of too, as if the women have offset all costs of delivery and post-delivery. Nobody is denied treatment or attention simply because she has no money.

However, a very embarrassing situation emerges thereafter, when these women not are discharged from the hospital till all bills are offset by them or their relatives. They are detained in separate reserved small rooms as they are indebted to the hospitals. In some cases, women from very poor families spend up to nine months in the hospitals' detention rooms with their new babies. To avoid this embarrassing situation, women usually go against doctors' advice of vagina deliveries in the labour rooms since the bills therefrom are much cheaper than those of cesarean sections. That is, they risk indirect demand for deaths. In some cases, the relatives might go borrowing to offset the direct costs of treatments for mothers and babies. In these cases, the burdens linger as they would need to work hard for a long time to be able to pay their debts.

I believe that all the poor women diagnosed not to be able to go through the normal process of vagina deliveries can be funded fully by public tax. There is always a threshold to determine who is a core poor. I further believe that if this is done, maternal morbidity and mortality would be greatly reduced, as many women who do not want to enter the theater rooms and still prefer the labour rooms are mostly afraid of the bills therefrom.

The managements of the hospitals have endeavoured to institute an indigent fund to which some public spirited individuals and organizations donate. From these funds, the hospitals manage to offset some of the costs of treatments for these women on the basis of First Come First Serve. Dr. Philip Ugbodaga, herein referred to as Doc. Phil for the love I have for him, a former Edo State Chairman of Nigerian Medical Association said:

"Hospital managements can, for the sake of these patients, contact some civil organizations with a view to bailing the women out, as I did during my tenure as the Managing Director of the Edo State owned Central Hospital".

Unfortunately too, the government has not formerly recognized these funds instituted by the various hospitals or proposed special methods of contributing to these funds. Anyway, the hardship that has spared nobody in Baba Bubu's administration has almost gnarled these funds. No matter how crude this model may seem; that the mothers are not allowed to celebrate their joy of motherhoods till their bills are paid by someone, it is still advantageous over the Out-of-Pocket model. The first and chief of them is that lives are saved irrespective of income and insurance status. All complicated cases are treated without abandoning both mothers and babies to die because of poverty. The relatives of the women have enough time to work and gradually offset the bills, as the hospitals allow payments in installments. In a few cases, patients get money from the indigent funds, and public spirited individuals on humanitarian visits to the hospitals also take up some of the bills.

The government and the international health concerns must step in because no woman should die in the process of bringing another life to this world, when the country is blessed with very good gynecologists. No child who could become the best president of the country should die from minor infant diseases that can easily be resolved by the very good pediatricians in the country. No old person who has served the country diligently should die of minor age-related diseases that can easily be resolved by the very good geriatricians in the country.

Will the government take the managements of the hospitals serious in order to cover the identified existing gaps in this observed model? No, forget it in the Baba Bubu regime. His Minister of Health does not even know that such a thing exists in the hospitals because he does not care to know. They only know about the campaigns against the highly infectious diseases of global concern, like the Covid-19, in which they can divert millions of monies in different currencies to their private accounts. They would be compelled to have enough budgets for health if only the western countries can help deny them and their children access to healthcare abroad since they only fear Britain and America, not their citizens.

For the avoidance of doubt, the other existing healthcare models, mostly practiced by countries that are concerned about the lives of their citizens such as in Baba Bubu's London are: (i) "The Beveridge Model", formulated in 1948 and named after William Beveridge, a reformer and designer of the National Health Service system in Britain. In the model, the government uses tax payments to finance and provide healthcare in much the same way it provides security and public library. Most hospitals and clinics are owned by the government, doctors are employees of the government even though there are some who are not, but collect their fees from the government. Nobody gets any doctor's bill and the government, as a sole payer, is in control of what a doctor can charge. (ii) "The Bismarck Model", named after the Prussian Chancellor, Otto Von Bismarck, the man who invented the welfare state, as part of the effort to unify Germany in the 19th century. It is

Social Health Insurance founded in 1883. There is a pre-existing "sickness fund", which is the insurer in an insurance system. This fund is financed by the employers and employees through deduction from payrolls. Doctors and hospitals are mostly private and there is tight regulation, which gives the government more control and to device a way to cover everybody, though it is to keep workers healthy for productivity. (iii) "The National Health Insurance (NHI) Model", which has both elements of the Beveridge and Bismarck models. Private sector providers are used, but only the government runs insurance programmes, which every citizen pays into. There is no need for marketing, and as such, no financial intention to deny claims and there is no profit. The universal insurance programmes are cheaper and much simple to administer than the Bismarck model, where insurance is for profit.

The NHI model was introduced in Nigeria by Baba Obasara about 19 years ago but till now, the coverage is still not up to six percent of the population; only few among the working class are covered. What a shame! The coverage of the NHI model can remain as low for a very long period in the country because unlike in Canada, there is a very large informal sector as in a developing country like Nigeria, which cannot easily be captured. It would be difficult to track the many artisans and the huge jobless population in the labour surplus economy of Nigeria. This is especially so among the inhabitants of the rural areas who mostly have access to only the limited and underfunded primary healthcare system. A serious government would task public health researchers on what to do about this ugly situation. A serious Medical Association or union would brain a way forward and hold the government to account rather than striking for wage increase all the time. However, nobody would mind them because Nigerian growth and development policies are not based on research and development. They are based on political considerations and whatever the politicians think about the rest of us.

The American government adopts all the three improved models. They used the United Kingdom's Beveridge model for their veterans; use the German Bismark model for their workers and use the Canadian National Health Insurance model for their senior citizens. Can anyone point to any reason why the citizens of such a country would not be patriotic or think of the country first? Again, is that not one of the inheritances of the American youth, for which J. F. Kennedy had told them not to think of what America would do for them but what they could do for America, which Nigeria lazy leaders have twisted and have been singing about? How would a youth in Nigeria whose dear mother has died from a minor ailment because of poverty ever think of his country first?

Chapter Fifteen

Upon Baba Bubu's Return

One would have thought that upon Baba Bubu's return from his long sickness leave and his occasional resuscitation trips from the London hospital, he would be challenged replicate the technologies to which he now owes his life in a country he was elected to govern. He had made a heartwarming revelation to country men, on how technologies had restored back his health. He had confessed that he never knew how important technology could be in saving lives. That was a big relief to stakeholders in the health sector. They had believed that as a patient who had had a firsthand experience of the effects of technology in healthcare production and delivery, the President would rise to the occasion. Yet, Nigerian hospitals have at best, obsolete machines and equipment. That is a country led by a man who took an oath to safeguard the lives of his countrymen and had seen for the first time that machines can play such a role in healthcare delivery. Yet, he could not take technology in healthcare production as a challenge in his country. No. His most serious challenge is to rediscover all grazing routes in the country, to facilitate his most important but obdurate and pigheaded task in government; to ensure the land conquest agenda of the Fulani. If only technology could do that for him.

He now roves about countries, seeking healthcare, just to stay alive. Each time he is diagnosed with accumulated diseases and resuscitated, his handlers would quickly organize his public appearances; to say one or two things to his country people before his bad health goes worse again. This became the trick till they decided to permanently import doctors from the United Kingdom and Saudi Arabia for his daily resuscitation. This has only reduced his visits to the London hospital.

For failing to replicate what he had experienced in London hospital to at least, one hospital in his country (as compensation for his failed promise never to seek healthcare abroad if the ordinary citizens of his country could not), he is not only treacherous but also a monumental catastrophe. For a man who once said that there was no difference between the elected government officials and the electorates, how is it that till now, he goes so often to London for healthcare when the electorates cannot? How is it that only him, his family, and a few cliques who have laid hold to the nation's wealth are the ones who can purchase quality health? There is no government office where outlawing medical tourism is a debate any longer, simply because it has become a routine for the President. The debate once raised on whether foreign medical trips should be banned or not, to which he was once in the affirmation, had died down among the stakeholders and legislators, simply because the President has become a sicklier. He is now infested with diseases to which no doctor or herbalist has a cure at home.

How can it be explained to generations of Africans that once upon a time, it was sickness, and not to improve the image of a country or to bring in investments that mostly made their most populous nation's president traveled the world and met the world class doctors? Yet, he was unable to recognize and attract them to his country? Who would dare name his child after the President any longer? Not even the Nigerian Fulani who would have realized the great disservice Baba Bubu had done unto them.

It is probably that the President has come to believe that the country owes him and his Fulani tribe a lot of debt. Or that he had come to envy the loots of Gen. Sani Abacha and as such, needs the opportunity to grab his share of the commonwealth, and build for himself the so called "dynasty" before he joins his ancestors. He may be very angry with the people for refusing to elect him as the President on time, or when he actually needed it; for he had publicly regretted that he did not become the President at the right age. So, his anger is now on the people for delaying his destiny. So, if the Fulani agenda is the only thing he could still accomplish, the presidency is still worth it.

Only if he were really a man who had sympathy for even his poor Fulani people roaming about the bushes! He now roams to and fro the routes of the world like the devil, devouring the nation's collective wealth, battling to stay alive. Like the devil, he could not imagine that so many poor people daily carry along with them, the burdens of unknown several diseases as he does. Those people are never his concerns. His only concerns are himself and his family, and then, the health of cows, and not even that of his Fulani tribal men. By extension, his cabinet members have also restricted their health and education concerns to themselves and members of their families. This has gone down the ladder, with no one to care for public health and education in the country. Any doctor or lecturer, irrespective of whatever training he has, no matter how good, who is tired of the country, can simply leave. The Minister of Labour has publicly said so because anybody in the government under a sick president can say or do anything. The only time they mind the doctors or lecturers when they are on strike is when it interferes with their political lives.

My childhood friend in America called me in my dreams; to inform me that he has decided to take America as his country. That is, he is no longer a Nigerian. He had gone to America years before; upon the completion of his National Youth Service Corps. He left with the high hope that he would return to build a house for his mother and bring her out of poverty; at least, the community starts from the family unit. Now, he has reversed his decision. Instead, he has relocated his mother to America, where she would not only be housed as an elderly woman or a senior citizen but also has good medical care and enjoy her life as a human being.

"Does that not amount to a loss of your generation in Africa", I asked, knowing that he is the only son of his father.

"How", he asked.

"Your father begot you in Africa, who will you beget in Africa?"

"I do not care about that. They have messed up that country beyond repair".

"But America is other people's country, not yours".

"Who are the other people? That is how different people came to America and become citizens. We have African-Americans, Asian-Americans, and so on. Yet, unlike in your country, Nigeria, no one group is empowered by the government to kill other groups simply because a man from the group is the President."

"But insecurity is also in America. What of the September 11th 2001 attack on World Trade Centre?" I asked, repeating after the country's infamous Minister of Information.

"I was not in America then. Since I came to America, I have never heard of such an attack. In your country, it is every now and then, again and again with dozens and scores of people dying and I wonder how people still survive there. Then, your president is happy that people are dying, provided they are not from his ethnic group but he would do everything to protect the cows. The police deployed to combat cattle rustling are better trained and equipped than those deployed to combat criminalities and killings. Your president gives tactical support to the rampaging Fulani herdsmen to destroy farms, rape women, and kill people. I can no longer belong to a country where the lives of cattle and cows are more important than the lives of human beings", he concluded.

He wrote to me later that he has transferred the begetting issue I had raised to America. He believed that if his father had known what would become of Nigeria and had the choice, he would have begotten his son in America in the first place. So, wherever his father is now, he should be proud that his son has corrected his mistake of begetting his only son in Nigeria. He criticized my idea of working hard and making it in Nigeria because the President does not believe in the youth of the country, let alone encourage hard work. He challenged me to point to any serious programme deliberately emplaced to encourage any hard working Nigerian youth other than constituting them as an unemployed army for dirty jobs, and I found virtually none. He told me that the President and the leaders of the country know what they are doing; for they all have sent their precious children to America as their real home because they do not believe in Nigeria as a country. So, he wondered why on earth he too should have the opportunity to do for himself what the President and his cohorts do for their children and refuse to do so. This left me speechless and defeated.

"Your president believes that all youths except those who move from one bush to another with cattle and cows are lazy", he said.

It pained me that I would be losing a childhood friend forever; only to be seen in my dream. I thank God for creating dreams; for in there, I had seen my lost loved ones. I have seen my great grandmother (actually an aunt), Eselebor, the old woman who brought me up and died in her nineties when I just completed my National Youth

Service Corps (she did not wait for any reward). She is the woman who those people who think I am stubborn and behave "anyhow" need to query; another aunty, Ebeagbor; my precious cousin, Esther; my first friend on earth, Monday and my benefactor, Chief Anenih.

My American friend is a sharp guy; a brain and a first class product of a foremost university in the country, who I believe could have combined with others to bring the country out of poverty. Now, as part of their deliberate incentive policies to encourage quality human capital and mobilize human resources into the country, America has given him an offer he could not reject. He has become a made in Nigeria first class product for the use of America. Does Baba Bubu's government have any concern about any brain drain and brain gain? As a big player in Africa, does the country under the President has any concern for brain circulation within the region? The government believes that anybody who is tired of living in the country should simply excuse them and go to wherever he likes and never return, instead of disturbing the President with stories. Does it not take only intelligence to recognize intelligence and what the country can benefit from intelligent people? Does it not take only a brain to recognize a brain? Now that we have a brainless man as the President, it might just be rational for the brain to give him a chance because of the problem of incompatibility.

I cannot wholly blame my friend who has sought a better life and opportunity to realize his full potentials. It is the Nigerian government that does not know what to do in order to harness the advantages of globalization I should blame. The government is only boastful that the country's International Airports are busy. It does not care whether it is busy for injection or for leakage of the economy. As long as the emigration does not affect cows and the roads are opened for the immigration of Fulani herdsmen from any part of the world, to join in the fight for lands conquest and expansionist agenda, his understanding of migration is complete. There is even now a deliberate plan to encourage the rich non-Fulani families to send their children out of the country, in the guise of schooling, in order to reduce the competition with future Fulani generations and facilitate the proper takeover of the land, which they said God has given them. Imagine! The Ijaw people who were the first tribe to enter Nigeria have not claimed any God's given land.

It has now become a common prayer point in all churches and mosques that God should take care of the victims of the Fulani herdsmen, kidnappers, and bandits; even if the particular criminals may not be Fulani herdsmen. These were atrocities that were only heard of in the Far East by Nigerians in time past. What a shameless president? Again, who would rescue our Nigerian Fulani brothers from this Baba Bubu's inflicted stigma?

May God have mercy on His people.

PART TWO

In this part of the book, I compiled some of the thought provoking speeches, news items, and positions or events of prominent Nigerians, as they were published, and make my comments on them. I do not know for sure whether these are the true words of those persons to whom the words were attributed or not. What I do know is that things have so fallen apart in the country that non state actors are now more trusted by the citizens than the government they had elected. In any case, I consider them to be true reflections of the situation in the country, as occasioned by the President's administration. Recent events in the country have provoked them, making them worth my dreams and my comments.

1. *"From "Cattle Colony" to "Grazing Routes" to "Grazing Reserves" to "RUGA" to "National Livestock Transformation Plan" to "Historic Cattle Routes" to "Farm Estates". For 6 years, how can the main policy drive of a presidential administration be focused on cows?*

For 6 years, there have been different attempts by the Buhari administration to collect lands from indigenous people and hand them over to herdsmen, making the lands officially belong to the nomads. Why is the Federal Government hell bent on sponsoring the personal businesses of a particular ethnic group?"

- Gurumwal George Longjan

My Comment

The President is not hell-bent on sponsoring any business. He is only hell-bent on conquering lands for his ethnic group; the Fulani, as he had promised them. Sadly, most of them are not even Nigerians. If he were hell bent on sponsoring their businesses, he would have easily succeeded. He would have coarse the Central Bank of Nigeria into them giving grants or zero-interest loans. He would have helped them to build ranches across the willing states and create jobs for their teeming youths. No, to the President, nothing is worth it if it would not conquer land for the Fulani. That is only where Nigerians are resisting him. So far, he has only succeeded in sending them to wars in which they have been killed more than any ethnic group while he and his family roll from country to country in search of health and comforts.

Again, it was the agreement the President had reached with his Fulani tribe anywhere they are found. That is why the Fulani criminals are being protected while the peaceful Fulanis are left vulnerable to be attacked because the President does not see a non-violent Fulani as a true Fulani. Any security officer who likes his job would better not parade the violent Fulani. The other day, a group of kidnappers was arrested; one of them raised the alarm that the Fulani men among them were not paraded with them. A Fulani serial killer who was remanded by a court in a prison in Oyo State was found never to have been there upon the jailbreak, and the prison officer had nothing to explain. However, the President forgets that the minority can never lord it over the vast majority in war, no matter how they try. I can assure you that the land conquering agenda will never work.

---

2. As Nigeria is collapsing around us, let us remember how we got here.

ROLL CALL OF THE PROMOTERS OF FAILURE IN NIGERIA

Here are some of the prominent names that helped send BUHARI to Aso Rock:

1. Dr. Oby Ezekwesili
2. Fela Durotoye
3. Atiku Abubakar
4. Omoyele Sowore
5. Izala Muslim clerics and Christian clerics.
6. Chief Olusegun Obasanjo
7. Professor Charles Soludo
8. Pastor Tunde Bakare
9. Pastor Sunday Adelaja

10. *Father Ejike Mbaka*
11. *Professor Pastor Yemi Osibanjo*
12. *Professor Tam David West*
13. *Professor Wole Soyinka*
14. *Rev. Chris Okotie*
15. *Professor Pat Utomi*
16. *Nasir El-Rufai*
17. *Dino Melaye*
18. *Lai Mohammed*
19. *Rochas Okorocha*
20. *Rotimi Amaechi*
21. *Adams Oshiomhole*
22. *Dr. Bukola Saraki*
23. *Aminu Tambuwal*
24. *Bola Ahmed Tinubu*
25. *Raji Fashola*
26. *Dr. Chris Ngige*
27. *Rabiu Kwankwaso*
28. *Ibikunle Amosun*
29. *Rauf Aregbesola*
30. *Kayode Fayemi*
31. *Sanusi Lamido*
32. *Deacon Femi Adesina*
33. *Pastor E. A Adeboye*
34. *Pastor W. Kumuyi*
35. *Dr. Ogbonnaya Onu*
36. *Kenny Ogungbe*
37. *Dato Adeneye*
38. *Magnus Abbey*
39. *Dakuku Peterside*
40. *9ice*
41. *Kenny St. Ogungbe Brown*

42. *Tunde Disu*
43. *John Momoh*
44. *Maupe Ogun*
45. *Chamberlain Usoh*
46. *Suleiman Aleide*
47. *Monday Onyekachi Ubani*
48. *Iffy Ubani*
49. *Labourous Osuoma*
50. *Citizen Useni Jones (Radio continental 102.3FM).*
51. *Joe Igbokwe*
52. *Dele Momodu*
53. *Abike Dabiri*
54. *Professor Attahiru Muhammadu Jega*
55. *Muazu*
56. *Emeka Ojukwu Jnr.*
57. *Egenti E. Raymond (Ogudo)*
58. *Victor Umeh*
59. *Wasiu Ayinde (Kwam 1)*
60. *T. Y. Danjuma*
61. *Lauretta Onochie*
62. *Jide Kosoko*
63. *Jonah David Jang*
64. *MC Oluomo and his NURTW men*
65. *Solomon Dalung*
66. *Naja'atu Mohammed*
67. *Buba Galadima*
68. *Oba of Lagos, Oba Akiolu*
69. *Shehu Sanni*
70. *Desmond Eliott*
71. *Femi Kuti*
72. *George Udom*

These people and the entire RCCG actually believed that Buhari had what it takes to lead Nigeria into a first world. These people went to school. Many are Professors. Some claimed to have direct access to God. Some are gifted with "prophecies." They read history. They understood international relations. They understood how societies work or so we thought. They were more than 20 years old in 1983 when Buhari shot himself to power. They saw Buhari murder innocent Nigerians in 1983. They saw Buhari destroy the economy in 1983. They saw the role Buhari played in Abacha's government.

They read all the threats of violence by Buhari against the nation. They saw Buhari harass Lam Adesina the Oyo State Governor due to Fulani herdsmen's conflicts with locals in Oyo State. They saw Buhari led the sharia protest that claimed the lives of innocent Nigerians in 2001. They saw Buhari and his minions open the gate of hell on innocent Nigerians when he lost the presidential election in 2011.

If Buhari was not speaking and defending his Fulani heritage, he would be fighting to defend his religious heritage. Never for once did he defend Nigeria or give an interview on how to rebuild the economy, education, power, health, etc. They saw everything this man did. They knew him too well to miss the little details of his violent life. But they were united in hatred for Goodluck Ebele Jonathan. Jonathan was one among the few Nigerian leaders that actually wanted Nigeria to work.

Hatred became a unifying force to push forward a false narrative. They exploited his humility. They exploited his kindness. They exploited his humanity. They danced and made merry in Ojota. They ate, drank and danced away the destiny of a nation.

- Unknown Author

My Comment

I think that number 24 should have been number 1 on this list, if the role they played was anything to go by. He was the prime mover who resurrected the a dead ambition in the first place before any other person became a controlled factor. I know that many of them were desperate for power but I am not quite sure that all of them did it for the hatred of Goodluck Ebele Jonathan. I think human infallibility played a role. The President is only a failure, with sadness and ethnic vengeance dwelling in his heart, and according to Atiku Abubakar, Nigeria has never been so bad in his more than seventy years of life. I am sure so many of them have regretted it. At least, Dino Melaye has publicly apologized on behalf of all those who "fired blind shots". The only problem now is that they have not told us about the plans to reawaken those who were killed or put to permanent disability positions by their shots"

---

3. *Mark My Words, War Will Soon Break Out in Nigeria"*

"Another civil war in Nigeria has become imminent and inevitable. The reason for its inevitability is simply because Muhammadu Buhari, the Northern Nigeria Fulani oligarchs and the wider network of Fulani in Sub-Saharan Africa have concluded plans to adopt Nigeria as the homeland for all Fulani in Africa.

Fulani have realized that the wandering and rootless lifestyle of cattle herding is no longer tenable in the twenty-first century. Fulani needs to have land to call home and rear cattle and that land should be Nigeria. The indigenous peoples of Nigeria have clearly, vehemently and stridently opposed this diabolic plan and both sides are mobilizing for war.

The Fulani won't relent and the indigenous people will not give up their land.

The same Fulani Project, having failed so shamelessly and woefully in the Central African Republic, will not be allowed to fail this time as the Nigerian Fulani project is better funded with the massive [stealing] of the sovereign wealth of Nigeria through nationwide kidnapping for ransom by lower class Fulani and the seizure of the reins of Government and wealth by the elite Fulani.

Kidnapping and the seizure of the institutions of Government are all for the purpose of implanting Fulani into the mainstream and control of politics and the economy of Nigeria for the objective of funding the Fulani Project in Nigeria.

The Central African Republic (CAR) has gone through the exact same experience that Nigeria is going through right now in the hands of the Fulani. The country has been run down by the killings and destitution wrought by rival gangs in the fight to destroy the chokehold the Fulani had on the politics and economy of their country. Although the Fulani hegemony over the CAR has been defeated, the street gangs that defeated the armed forces have turned on one another and themselves, unable to rise above petty gang warfare to rebuild their nation.

The Fulani have become blight on Africa and its biggest country Nigeria. Unable to break out of its centuries old cow herding and wandering culture, it continues to pull down every nation wherever it has any population. Some countries in West Africa, Ghana and their ancestral home Guinea have mastered the brutal tactics of dealing with Fulani and the Fulani have learned the bitter lesson by staying away from these countries.

In the CAR, the Fulani following the pattern of their ethnocentric politics had seized control of the commanding heights of the country's military and financial institutions, the foreign exchange trade, the mining and export of gold and above all the governing structures of Government. Mitchel Djotodia, a hare brained military officer and his Fulani faction seized power in a brazen coup by a demographic minority. All the non-Fulani military officers were flushed out of the forces, all the mineral deposits in the country were seized by Fulani merchants, non-Fulani traders were barred from trading in foreign exchange and the entire top echelon of the Civil Service were occupied by Fulani by as much as 83%.

France, the former colonial masters of CAR watched them do all these over the years and did not raise a protest. As in Nigeria, the Fulani were just 3% of the population of CAR, tucked in the desert recesses of the nation's Northwest. No world or regional power raised a whimper even though the ethnic groups of the rich southern forest regions roiled.

In CAR, the Fulani went even beyond the provocative as they are doing now in Nigeria.

They started seizing ethnic lands, raiding churches and killing worshippers, the most brazen being the attack on

Our Lady of Fatima Catholic Church in a town near Bangui the capital, where dozens of Catholic faithful were massacred during mass. The Fulani used their cattle bases allotted by Government to launch attacks and gunfights on the surrounding communities for robberies and ransom paying kidnaps as is happening now in Nigeria.

Again, as is happening in Nigeria today, the purpose of all the actions of the Fulani was simple; to transfer all wealth available in the CAR by all and every means and place it in the hands and control of the Fulani.

FULANI REPEATING IN NIGERIA WHAT THEY DID IN C.A.R.

The same playbook used in the Central African Republic is guiding the actions and policies of the Buhari Government in Nigeria.

1). The Fulani elite are raiding the Central Bank, buying dollars and other currencies at heavily discounted rates.

2). Other Fulanis are raiding the NNPC, plowing through the vaults and trading Nigerian crude for personal gain.

3). The educated wing is mowing down governing structures, taking forceful charge and control of all commanding heights of government and the armed forces.

4). The uneducated Fulani herdsmen are engaged in kidnapping for ransom and are now primed to take over ethnic lands, spreading themselves across the nation in settlements acquired with public funds to terrorize indigenous populations.

HOW THE YOUTH OF C.A.R. DESTROYED THE FULANI PROJECT

It will be of great use to retell the story of the Central African Republic so as to have an understanding of how the youth of the country removed the yoke of unremitting oppression by the Fulani. The youth formed street gangs and committed to taking on the army with all their vaunted training and intimidating and deadly weaponry. The youth had locally fabricated flint guns and machetes, while the army was menacing with their machine guns, grenade throwers and rocket launchers.

When the fight started on that fateful day in 2013 in Bangui, everyone expected a complete annihilation of the youth on the streets but the youth took the fight straight to the Guard Brigade near the Presidential Palace.

By the evening of the same day, soldiers' bodies were seen littering the streets while some were cut to pieces. By nightfall, the streets of Bangui had become the playground and the killing field of the youth of Bangui. In 3 days of street fighting, the entire Presidential Guards of the army of the CAR was decimated, in disarray running to their ethnic base in the far north and President Djotodia, the Fulani tyrant had abdicated and run away from the Presidential Palace and Capital, Bangui.

Tyrants survive for only as long as the people live in fear and choose to tolerate them. The Buhari Government is counting on deploying the Nigerian armed forces against the many ethnicities where the RUGA will be sited, beginning with the minority groups.

Buhari's plan is to deploy Nigerian troops to subdue Nigerian people for the benefit of Fulani. The central African Republic provides a veritable lesson on how to deal with the unrelenting Fulani menace. The Niger-Delta and Boko Haram if anything have shown that the Nigerian army is not invincible in a fight with local forces. If anything, the Nigerian Army will likely disintegrate if made to fight on many fronts at once.

It is a known truth that the Fulani will not relent in their quest for the conquest of Nigeria until they have seized all sources of income and made everyone else subservient to their rule and hegemony.

The Fulani in Nigeria, in nearly a century of political and economic ascendancy, have acquired so much power and money that it will defeat the purpose of such acquisition if they don't deploy it for the very purpose for the grasp for power, which is the conquest of Nigeria for the overlordship of the Fulani.

The final stage of the grand plan to subdue Nigeria for Fulani overlordship is afoot and Buhari and his people cannot back out now. So, a war has to be fought to resolve matters.

Our people say that you don't strip a woman naked just to start looking. Nigeria has been stripped naked and with the RUGA monstrosity in the works, the next thing is to start the deployment of troops to protect RUGA in their various locations of development.

It was bound to happen that the Fulani who have been taking so much out of Nigeria and have succeeded in binding Nigeria hand and foot politically and economically, will take the wrong step into the abyss one day. The logical culmination of all the rapaciousness would be the last ditch attempt at the ultimate land grab, to seize the lands belonging to indigenous communities and hand it over to Fulani.

Internecine war in different RUGA locations and different fronts is therefore inevitable. Communities will rage to keep their land or lose it to their eternal shame and regret. Communities, particularly in Igboland will rather choose to be annihilated than lose their land to hostile and predatory people.

Fulani has no land in Nigeria because they are not indigenous to Nigeria. They are migrants into Nigeria.

The decision by the Fulani to seize land by force in Nigeria can only lead to war in the many places where this seizure will happen. The people must resist as of necessity. They have done so in the Central Africa Republic and reduced the country to rubble and they will do it again in Nigeria.

Buhari will be compelled to deploy police and soldiers to defend the settlements and war will be declared everywhere there is a RUGA settlement in Nigeria. Fulanis have no land to hold dear and protect in Nigeria. In fact, Fulani have no stake or investment in the project called Nigeria and will not care if Nigeria burns. In fact, Fulani will be very willing to let Nigeria burn if the people are not willing to submit to their overlordship.

So they are minded to adopt a scorched earth policy to obliterate Nigeria. They have nothing to lose. They did it in CAR and they will do the same in Nigeria. It will be the responsibility of the indigenous people of Nigeria to find common grounds to protect the land of their ancestral inheritance and prevent the Fulani from putting a knife on their unity and their need to bind themselves together in one nation, but they cannot do this without first containing the Fulani. Fulani will try to divide them.

Buhari and the Fulani oligarchs are counting strongly on deploying the armed forces to quell insurrections that will arise from this massive land grab, but that will be the Achilles heel of their grand plan. Once soldiers are armed to put down these insurrections, they will turn against their commanders to defend their communities. Nigerians should therefore await the great unraveling of their armed forces.

Do the Fulani have the firepower, the men and the capacity to fight? In the entire history of the Nigerian armed forces, the Hausa/Fulani officers and enlisted men have always been promoted far beyond their qualifications and competencies. The capacity to fight and man the different departments of modern warfare will be put to the overwhelming test in any ensuing encounter.

The Fulani never fight an enemy in frontal war. They attack isolated and undefended villages. In any direct confrontation, they run away. It was evident even in the battle of Bangui. Well-armed Fulani soldiers could not take on street gangs with flint guns and machetes. It has also shown in the war against Boko Haram. The poor performance of commanders of their ethnic stock is a bad joke among soldiers in the front.

Hausa/Fulani soldiers had to be sorted out and protected from slaughter by Boko Haram forces. This is not to talk of unending betrayals of their Christian colleagues and commanders in the battlefront.

Buhari, a Fulani irredentist, will use to his and for the benefits of his agenda to divide, the ethnic and religious cleavages among the people of Nigeria. But the people ought to know that the Fulani are friends to no one and that a Fulani friend today can become an adversary tomorrow.

You are only friend to Fulani for as long as you continue to serve a purpose in their overall plan.

Let the talk cease and the battle begins.

Copied! Please share widely with the whole southwest, southeast, south, and middle belt because there is nothing like north central according to the 1994 constitutional conference.

–Olusegun Obasanjo

My Comments

Before he became the President of Nigeria, not many actually hated the Fulani because they were only as criminals as any other Nigerian. If the President had any atom of love for them, he would have genuinely found solutions to this nomadic life of his ethnic group. He should not have exposed their nakedness to the majority of the people. Right now, nobody loves the Fulani herdsmen in a country where they were once a delight to meet by the villagers on the bush path. The President has made their anathemas. Who would rescue them after him?

Yes, Baba, you get it right. However, the agenda is dead on arrival. The President probably thought that he could easily pass those various laws he had proposed to enable his Fulani agenda, but he has seen for himself now that it is not easy to subdue a very sophisticated nation like ours. No matter how sturdy the minority tribe is, it can never have its way over the majority in war. Baba, just as they did not succeed in CAR, they would not succeed here; Nigeria will be more hellish for them if they start. How do you think a Yoruba soldier would be deployed to go and protect the Fulani's interest in any Yoruba land? Let us not talk of the

Igbo soldier. How many are the Fulani to fight such a civil war across the country when the entire south and the middle belt have long realized that Col. Ojukwu was after all, right.

The Fulani have already realized that the war is lost. The regional and sub-regional security forces or vigilantes are actually preparations for this envisaged wars, and with their experience in CAR, some senses have entered them. They have resorted to kidnapping and banditry for big money, so that when the President must have left office, they too would live like their elites, instead of the continuous nomadic lives. They can only enjoy it while it lasts; as long as their chief patron is in power.

However sir, you were one of those who brought this misfortune upon us simply because you hated his predecessor. You have not apologized to us. So, we all shall live with it; those of us who would survive this stormy time would tell the story.

---

4. *GENERAL YAKUBU GOWON'S ADVICE TO BUHARI...*

"There was corruption in Nigeria when Awolowo built Cocoa House, TV station and the first University in Africa

There was corruption in Nigeria when IBB built Third Mainland Bridge, built Aso Rock, National Assembly Complex, turned Abuja into our Federal Capital Territory.

There was corruption in Nigeria when Obasanjo brought GSM, banking reform, police reform, and civil defense, There was corruption in Nigeria when Jonathan introduced BVN and PVC, built 12 new Federal Universities, revamped railway lines, made our economy fastest growing in Africa & third in the world.

Great leaders don't blame people and events for their failures. They simply accept responsibility and move on. What has the President done after all the promise of fixing power in six weeks, reducing pump price to 45 Naira, making N1 equal to $1, stopping Boko Haram, etc? It's a shame.

The truth is, corruption started from heaven when Satan violated a privilege given him. That never stops God's works.

He waited for God to create man and brought his lawlessness and corruption into the Garden of Eden.

God wasn't moved. He introduced a redemption plan; The Saviour was born, sadly, Judas Iscariot was there.

Not discouraged yet, He gave us God the Holy Spirit.

If anyone tells you the reason the President is not working is that he inherited corruption, tell them corruption is rooted in the DNA of Homo sapiens because we are just mere mortals infected with a virus of good & evil.

Yet, great leaders don't blame people and events for their failures. They simply accept responsibility and move on."

My Comments

Baba, and there was corruption when you ensured the implementation of a national economic development plan.

The President and his clique have no clue on how the economy works. They had thought that corruption was an economic policy. When his men were talking with passion about corruption before his election, I knew that they did not know what they were talking about. I knew that their idea of fighting corruption has nothing to do with technology but to throw away the baby and the bathe water. With his ignorance, The President exposed Nigeria to the predators of the world and placed the country permanently in the danger zone of globalization, strengthening Nigeria's disadvantaged destiny in the development matrix. We need him to leave the government in order to reset our agenda from his Fulani agenda. He would remain the worst President ever in the history of Nigeria.

---

5. MY PERSECUTION BY BUHARI REGIME: SETTING THE RECORDS STRAIGHT – Chief Sunday Adeyemo aka Igboho.
02 July 2021.

The invasion of my home by Nigerian security operatives and the Department of State Security's (DSS) announcement that I am wanted has made it essential for me to set the records straight for Nigerians and the international community.

Nigerian security operatives invaded my residence in the early hours of Wednesday, 1 July 2021. The invasion was done without a search warrant. I was not invited for questioning/investigation at any government facility before the invasion. The operatives that stormed my residence destroyed a lot of my property, killed persons and stole valuables and money. Pictures and videos of their atrocities have been widely reported in the media.

Nigerians and the world at large are aware of my resistance to the incessant killings, raping and kidnapping of my people in southwest Nigeria by armed Fulani herdsmen. The failure of the President and his government to curb the criminal activities of the murderous herdsmen necessitated my intervention. I ordinarily would not have intervened if the government had lived up to its responsibility of securing the southwest and Nigeria at large from the criminal activities of the President's ethnic men.

Of public knowledge, my intervention has not led to any loss of life or bloodshed. By means of curbing criminality is to chase the criminal Fulani herdsmen out of their hideouts in the company of the people of the affected communities. It is because of the foreseen government persecution that videos of such interventions were transmitted live on social media. Nigerians, the security operatives, and the presidency are aware that I have never moved against the peaceful Fulani and other tribes living peacefully in the southwest. My unjust persecution -- for defending my people and community -- is therefore surprising and unwarranted.

After several unsuccessful attempts to link me to any crime, the government desperately opts to forcefully silence me, so that the criminal herdsmen, who enjoy the government's sympathy, protection and immunity, can easily outrun the southwest. The presidency's aerial antics and desperation to acquire people's ancestral lands across Nigeria for foreign Fulani herdsmen because they share ethnicity and occupation with the President is well known to Nigerians and the international community. I am being seen as a threat to the Fulanization agenda in the southwest, hence the desperation to soil my name.

Nigerians and the international community should please be aware that the security operatives that invaded my home either planted the ammunitions being paraded in the media in my home or harvest them from their armoury to frame me. The arms paraded are not mine, they are government magic. I protect myself with traditional powers, not with guns.

The federal government framed me up and the sequence of events brings the truth bare. Why would the security agents invade my home at night and destroy my surveillance cameras before carrying out their operation if not that they had an ulterior motive? In this modern age of technological advancement, why did the security operatives not put on body cameras to record their activities from the point of entry to their time of exit? Their action is a testament that the government is incurable of using a desperate approach to silence peaceful social interventions.

The unwarranted military invasion of Lekki, gruesome killing of peaceful EndSARS protesters, and evacuation of their bodies on 20 October 2020 is still fresh in the mind of Nigerians. A similar approach was adopted during the invasion of my home. The security operatives killed scores and took away their bodies. The government would have declared that 'unknown gunmen' invaded my home if they had succeeded in killing me. Nigerians and the international community should beware that desperate efforts are being made to force those arrested to make implicating confession statements. I advise the DSS to desist from their unprofessional acts and devote such energy to eradicating insecurity.

Nigerians and the international community should please note that I am a law abiding citizen without blemish. I advise the President to, in the interest of Nigerians that voted him to power, order his henchmen to desist from using falsehood and unholy tactics to soil my name. Such energy should be devoted to taming the herdsmen and bandits freely committing heinous crimes across Nigeria with impunity because their kinsman is in power.

Yoruba people would not be demanding for a nation if the government had lived up to its responsibilities. Self-determination is not a crime and all efforts to silence us and acquire our ancestral land for local and foreign criminal herdsmen will fail. Many Ken Saro-Wiwa arose after the Nigerian government unjustly executed the non-violent activist. Those that emerged after him confronted the government and almost brought Nigeria to its knees. I am another Saro-Wiwa. Therefore, I advise President Buhari to learn from the mistake of past governments. I am not Nigeria's problem and should not be framed up or intimidated for contributing my quota to ensure peace reigns in my region and country.

-   Olayomi Koiki
Spokesman Chief Sunday Adeyemo
2nd July 2021

My Comments

Sunday, you do not get it. If you were even moving against the peaceful Fulanis and other tribes living in the southwest, you would have been the best friend of the President, deserving national honors and contracts. You moved against the President's foot soldiers, the killer Fulani and allowed his stubborn ones and "betrayals" - the peaceful Fulani- who refused to key into the war, to live in peace. That is exactly your offence because you want to prove that your southwest zone can live peacefully with those Fulani who the President sees as cowards and tractors of their progenitor in the occupy Nigeria agenda . Maybe you need to know that just as the President saw a man like the former President, Late Yar'dua as not a true Fulani, those peaceful Fulani are not true Fulani. You want to prove that you can defeat terrors of all the President Buhari's true Fulani and you expect him, their godfather and grand patron to fold his hands and watch you? No.

---

6. 'Nigeria cannot defeat the Igbo and Yoruba at the same time

The greatest thing Nigerians accomplished in the last thirty years was electing Mohammadu Buhari as the President. If he had lived and died without being the President, no one would push back when politicians fall over themselves to deliver tributes and call him the greatest President that Nigeria never had.

After six years of Buhari's administration and with only two more years to go, all is settled about the rhymes and stanzas of Buhari's elegy. Some thirty years from now, people will stone anyone who attaches "greatest" to any tribute at Buhari's funeral.

You may ask if anything is worth the cost of having Buhari as the President.

Before you do, there is another reason why his election was the greatest accomplishment of the Nigerian electorate in the last 30 years. If Buhari had not been President, if his incompetence had not been exposed to the uninitiated, Nigeria would have continued its zigzag path. The one-step-forward, two-step-backward trajectory would have continued unabated. Thus, Buhari helped the unstructured Nigeria to confront its foreseeable future. That is Buhari's first legacy.

Here is Buhari's second legacy: It may not be clear yet to the Fulani people, but Buhari's presidency has damaged them more than any other group in Nigeria. Buhari's inability to have an objective view of what leadership entails in a diverse country like Nigeria and his propensity to side with his Fulani people even when every donkey could see the bias undermined the Fulani deeply. He diminished whatever legitimate claim they have in what is clearly a fast moving degenerative Nigeria's structural carnage. The Fulani were better off in Nigeria six years ago than they are today. That is Muhammadu Buhari's second legacy.

In the context of Nigeria's nationhood, Buhari's second coming was a necessary evil: He came, he saw, and he hastened its ruination for everyone.

If Buhari had not been President, Nigeria would have been 'managing.' The Peoples Democratic Party of Goodluck Jonathan and Sambo Dasuki and Diezani Allison-Madueke would have been paying Dangote to rob Otedola, even as the country continued the slide down the valley of death. Buhari accelerated the collapse by taking the country on a bungee jump down the deepest part of the valley using a frayed rope.

The rope is breaking. Anyone with functioning ears can hear the splitting threads from miles away. High above the deepest part of the valley, Nigeria barely holds on to Buhari's back. Two things will happen: Either Nigeria loses its grip on Buhari's back and falls into the valley of death, or the rope rips and both Nigeria and Buhari plunge down the valley. Either way, death is the expected end.

The only miracle on the horizon is to get Nigeria to a place where it cannot fight the Igbo and the Yoruba nations simultaneously.

In a one-on-one fight, Nigeria may defeat any of its components. Nigeria may defeat the Igbo. Nigeria may run over the Yoruba. Nigeria may crush the Ijaw, the Ibibio, the Tiv, the Ijaw, the Kanuri, the Fulani, the Bachama, the Idoma, the Urhobo, etc. Nigeria cannot defeat the Igbo and the Yoruba at the same time. In a fight between Nigeria on one side and an Igbo-Yoruba alliance on the other, many ethnic minority groups will take the side of the alliance.

Whether the fight is in the physical or spiritual realm, whether it is in the democratic realm of the ideological realm, Nigeria has no chance of winning a fight against the combined forces of the Igbo and the Yoruba. For a table with three legs, one leg has no chance of keeping the table standing when the other two legs take a knee. The Igbo and Yoruba need to take a combined knee. That is the ultimate way to shake the table called Nigeria.

Nigeria needs to get to a point where it faces the prospect of fighting a united Igbo and Yoruba power. It needs to happen now. That reality needs to be clear, concrete, and ironclad. It is the only magic wand that can save Nigeria.

Is it easy to achieve? No. Is it possible? Yes.

What will it take to get Nigeria to that place where it risks fighting the Igbo and the Yoruba simultaneously?

The way to achieve this is for the Igbo and the Yoruba to embrace Thomas Jefferson's greatest philosophy. The man who drafted the U.S. Declaration of Independence said, "I admire the dreams of the future more than the history of the past."

The Igbo and the Yoruba must admire the dreams of the future more than the history of the past. They must do it not just for their children's children but also for all those children from East to West, North to South, trapped in prisons of mediocrity and death, which are the only gift of an unfair, unjust, and dysfunctional Nigeria.

The Igbo and the Yoruba owe this to future generations of the people currently trapped in Nigeria. It is their responsibility. Posterity will blame the Igbo and the Yoruba in Nigeria if they fail to catch the wave. Thanks to Buhari's misadventures, the awareness of today is total and overwhelming. Severe penalties await the Igbo and the Yoruba if they fail to act now and free unborn generations from the manacles of Muhammadu Buhari's.

Professor Akinyemi Onigbinde
Snr. Research Fellow
Institute of African Studies
University of Ghana
Accra, Ghana

My Comments

Professor, I have also written on the trajectory of Nigerians if the President was not elected. Nevertheless, we cannot thank God that he became the President, except that in everything, we must give thanks to God. The government is biting more than it can chew, forgetting that it will soon expire. They are only preparing the instruments for enemies after the reign of the President to persecute him. The killers Fulani herdsmen have long realized that he has failed them too. Hence, they have resorted to banditry to hold government rather than individuals to ransom and of course, to get their piece of the cake from their grand patron. So that if money is what they get from the government and the war, they would still understand and could relocate out of Nigeria. Professor, they cannot even defeat only the Igbos alone, if they killed Nnamdi Kanu, more dangerous agitators would emerge. For example, has the gorilla warfare ended now since they have incarcerated Nnamdi Kanu? Don't you know that those who would make Kanu's type of agitation is a mere show not yet born, if the right thing is not done?

I know you meant Nigeria cannot 'survive', not "defeat" fighting the two simultaneously.

---

7. See what @Aminu Sa'ad Beli wrote on his wall. Moving forward I will start promoting peaceful separation for healthy development.

SEPARATION IS NOT ABOUT WAR, IT HAS A PEACEFUL ASPECT.

In 1776, the USA split from the UK.

In 1830 Belgium separated from the Netherlands.

In 1965, Singapore split off from Malaysia.

In 2002, East Timor got split off from Indonesia.

In 1921, Ireland split off from the United Kingdom, and (possibly in the future) there will be secession of Scotland.

In 1944, Iceland split from Denmark with remarkable ease.

In 1905 Norway split from Denmark

In 1905, Norway and Sweden also peacefully split ways. One got the car. The other got the kids.

In 1947, the British India Dominion was partitioned into India n Pakistan.

In 1971, Bangladesh seceded from Pakistan.

In 1992-93, the two parts of Czechoslovakia agreed to each go their own way. Thus were born the Czech Republic and Slovakia after what has been named the "Velvet Divorce". About the same time, another kind of separation occurred, of course, in Yugoslavia. This one led to bloodshed.

In 1965, Singapore split from Malaysia for a variety of reasons, including religious (Malaysia is majority Muslim, Singapore isn't), ethnic/racial (Singapore has a very large majority Chinese population) and concerns over the Malaysian Bumiputra policy, which was (and is) basically a form of "Affirmative Action" for Muslim Malaysians - who make up the majority population in Peninsular Malaysia.

Ethiopia and Eritrea

Sudan and South Sudan are now separate countries

USSR is now broken down into several countries.

I see separation as an avenue for healthy competition for development as in the case of Singapore and Malaysia, India and Pakistan, Norway/Denmark/Switzerland.

In the case of Nigeria, I am sensing a healthy competitive development among the original component part, the North/West/East each making useful progress while competing with the others.

It is not about war after all there is nothing wrong for one to decide he is no longer comfortable with the union and therefore wants to opt-out.

LET US GIVE PEACE A CHANCE AND SEPARATE HONOURABLY.

This is worth sharing over and over again...

- British named them Burma. They rejected it, restructured & renamed themselves Myanmar.

- *British named them Upper Volta, but they rejected it, restructured, and renamed themselves Burkina Faso - Land of Incorruptible People.*
- *British named them Gold Coast, they rejected it, restructured, and renamed themselves Ghana.*
- *British named them Southern Rhodesia. They rejected it, restructured, and renamed themselves Zimbabwe.*
- *British named them Northern Rhodesia. They rejected it, restructured, and renamed themselves Zambia.*
- *British named them Tanganyika. They rejected it, restructured & renamed themselves Tanzania.*
- *Germans named them the colony of South West Africa. They rejected it, restructured, and renamed themselves Namibia.*
- *France named them Dahomey. They rejected it, restructured, and renamed themselves Benin.*
- *Belgium named them Zaire. However, they rejected it, restructured & renamed themselves Democratic Republic of Congo (DRC).*
- *Britain named a bunch of people - Nigeria. They rather kill to preserve it than restructure and give themselves a befitting new name.*

"It is only an animal that bears the name that is given to it by his enemy" (Proverb).

My Comments

They have just a little period left for them to accept restructuring, even if as their lesser evil. If they do not, the separation we all do not want would be like magic in their eyes. I do not support separation and many do not; even the agitators do not but it becomes their option since the right thing is not being done. Our oneness has a lot of advantages but the present structure is eroding those advantages. Restructuring, therefore, the saving grace. However, if separation is what they chose accept instead of restructuring, so will it be.

---

8. Knowledge is Power!!!

Global Cattle Business Facts and Figures:
*NIGERIA'S 36 STATES & FCT RANKED IN ORDER OF LAND SURFACE AREA (KM²)**
1. *Niger State 76,363KM²*
2. *Borno State 70,898KM²*
3. *Taraba State 54,473KM²*
4. *Kaduna State 46,053KM²*
5. *Bauchi State 45,837KM²*
6. *Yobe State 45,502KM²*
7. *Zamfara State 39,762KM²*
8. *Adamawa State 36,917KM²*
9. *Kwara State 36,825KM²*
10. *Kebbi State 36,800KM²*
11. *Benue State 34,059KM²*
12. *Plateau State 30,913KM²*
13. *Kogi State 29,833KM²*
14. *Oyo State 28,454KM²*
15. *Nasarawa State 27,117KM²*
16. *Sokoto State 25,973KM²*
17. *Katsina State 24,192KM²*
18. *Jigawa State 23,154KM²*
19. *Cross River State 20,156KM²*
20. *Kano State 20,131KM²*
21. *Gombe State 18,768KM²*

22. Edo State 17,802KM²
23. Delta State 17,698KM²
24. Ogun State 16,762KM²
25. Ondo State 15,500KM²
26. Rivers State 11,077KM²
27. Bayelsa State 10,773KM²
28. Osun State 9,251KM²
29. Federal Capital Territory 7,315KM²
30. Enugu State 7,161KM²
31. Akwa Ibom State 7,081KM²
32. Ekiti State 6,353KM²
33. Abia State 6,320KM²
34. Ebonyi State 5,670KM²
35. Imo State 5,530KM²
36. Anambra State 4,844KM²
37. Lagos State 3,345KM²

Anambra + Enugu + Abia + Imo + Ebonyi = 29,525KM²

Kogi = 29,833KM²

Ogun + Oyo + Osun + Ondo + Ekiti = 76,320KM²

Lagos = 3,345KM²

Niger alone = 76,363KM²

Niger State = Entire Southwest States - Lagos

The entire Southeast is a little less than Kogi State only.

The North has enough land for ranching and cattle colonies. If seriously harnessed, the North could become a powerful player in the global cattle and beef business...

GLOBAL CATTLE BUSINESS: FACT SHEET
A. Top 10 NATIONS in terms of cattle inventory (2017).
1. INDIA 303 million
2. BRAZIL 226 million

3. CHINA 100 million.
4. USA 93 million.
5. EU 89 million.
6. ARGENTINA 53 million
7. AUSTRALIA 27 million
8. RUSSIA 18 million
9. MEXICO 16 million
10. TURKEY 14 million.

B. TOP 10 MILK EXPORTERS
1. NEW ZEALAND $4.4 Billion
2. GERMANY $2.6 Billion
3. NETHERLANDS $1.9 Billion
4. FRANCE $1.5 Billion
5. The USA $1.4 Billion
6. BELGIUM $1.2 Billion
7. AUSTRALIA $852 Million
8. BELARUS $637 Million
9. The UK $569 Million
10. SAUDI ARABIA $556 Million

C. TOP 10 BEEF EXPORTING NATIONS (2016).
1. AUSTRALIA $5.6 Billion
2. The USA $5.2 Billion
3. BRAZIL $4.3 Billion
4. INDIA $3.7 Billion
5. NETHERLANDS $2.7 Billion
6. IRELAND $2 Billion
7. NEW ZEALAND $1.9 Billion
8. CANADA $1.5 Billion
9. URUGUAY $1.4 Billion
10. GERMANY $1.3 Billion

Additional Considerations:
1. *Nigeria is not among the top 20 nations in the global cattle business.*
2. *None of the top cattle producing nations create cattle colonies or engage in primitive cattle grazing. All the top cattle producing and exporting nations utilize modern technology and ranching methods to maximize production and profit.*
3. *Nigeria's cattle business requires a complete rethink now and not later, for posterity's sake.*

- Unknown Author

My Comments

Firstly, in the politics of big and small countries, land mass is not a criterion. In Demographic Economics, it is about the population and carrying capacity of a country, not mere land (Land Surface Area) with less population density. In Monetary and International Economics, it is about a country having a voice in the global price (and cartel) of its most important foreign exchange earning commodity. For all I know, that commodity is oil in Nigeria, not cattle.

Secondly, take your Arithmetic to the dustbin; so says the President's cabal. They only imitate America when it suits their selfish interests. Why would the President not imitate America in ranching? Why would he not patronize the United Kingdom as he does with his health? The President is not in to better the lots of his kinsmen in the true sense; otherwise, he could have made cow business lucrative for them. He can no long think; some people are just thinking for him. Their interest is to satisfy some of their ancestors. They have to fight for their age long agenda so that when they die, their ancestors would welcome them with open arms. They think more of how the President would be given a special place in paradise, as he journeys towards the abode of his ancestor while they flock around him as they arrive there one after the other. Yet, they did not ask themselves who would go there first, as in the case of the head of the cabal, the late Chief of Staff.

---

8. President Buhari Goofed on Southern Governors' Anti-Grazing Stance
By Chief Mike Ozekhome, SAN

President Muhammadu Buhari has obviously been ill-advised on the well thought out Southern Governors' stance against open grazing by the Attorney General whose views were made known only two days ago. Buhari, with all humility, is quite wrong to say the Southern Governors' stance is an act of questionable legality. If the Federal Government feels strong and sure about its puritanical, but legally flawed stance, I challenge the Federal Government to challenge the Governors' resolutions by suing all the State Governors of Nigeria, through the invocation of the original jurisdiction of the Supreme Court under section 232(1) of the 1999 Constitution. The action will fail miserably. I am ready, able and willing to defend such states "probono". I can state categorically that neither the president's views nor those of the Attorney General, are anchored on any provisions of the Constitution. The Constitution is the fons et origo, the ground norm, the Oba, Eze, Oghie and Emir of our laws. Other laws must bow to the supremacy of this National identity card of a country; for such other laws or FG's resistance are but mere warrant

Chiefs, Daudus, Bales, and Ukpi Drummers within the Constitution's sacred domain. The Governors have been given powers by the same Constitution in sections 5(2), 11(2), 14(2)(b), 176(2) and 215(4) of 1999

Constitution to act as the Chief Security Officers of their various States to provide their citizens with welfare and security, which the Constitution says are the primary purpose of government. The Houses of Assembly of the states have equally been given powers by section 4(7) of the same Constitution to make laws for peace, order, and good government in their states. In accordance with hallowed principles and practice of federalism and democracy, the Southern Governors do not require any permission from, or approval by, the FG for them to govern their states and protect their citizens, in the same way, a boarding house pupil must first seek his Headmaster-s permission to visit his parents outside the school. Mr. President's statement, churned out, as usual, by his SSA on Media and Publicity, Mr. Garba Shehu, to the effect that the Governors were politicking with serious security issues and attempting a show of power, is, therefore, most unfortunate, embarrassing, divisive, ethnocentric, insensate and insensitive to the memory of dead and dying Nigerians. These are thousands of innocent Nigerians savagely and brutally mauled down in cold blood, either in their own homes, farms, or on the streets and alleys, by these rampaging pastoralists. The President appears undisturbed and unperturbed that Nigerians, especially in the South, have their wives, mothers and daughters violently violated and raped by these marauding AK-47 riffles-wielding expansionists that wear the fake toga of herdsmen. What has the Government done about it? Nothing. It usually customarily wrigs its hands in pretended helplessness and washes them off every loss of life like Pontius Pilate in the Bible. This is so despicable!. It is so abhorrent and shameful! Only yesterday, 124 people were slaughtered in just three states, with 100 of them being children, women and the elderly in Benue State alone. Nigerians have become weary of mourning. The Governors are tired of being Chief mourners, undertakers and elegy poets of their citizens. And Buhari is saying they must shut up and worship on the blood-sucking alter of Nigeria's so-called unity, indivisibility and indissolubility? We are living a lie of a contraption called a country that has since been reduced to a big scam and a one-chance dilapidated vehicle on a drudgery journey to no destination. I challenge the Federal Government to go to the Supreme Court and challenge the states. By this, I hereby alter my earlier stance that the states should sue the Federal Government. No. It is the complaining and fretting FG that should take that step if uncomfortable with the Southern Governors' communiqué. The states should go ahead and enforce the anti-grazing laws in their respective domains, using their neighborhood and vigilante security outfits since (and I can bet on this), the FG will never lend its centrally - commanded Police Force to aid the states. It is so easy to predict this clueless Government from the negative. For emphasis, we are operating a federal system of government, not a unitary system. The Federal Government cannot, therefore, dictate to states like a slave owner to his purchased slaves. It is an aberration. Freedom of movement and the right of some Nigerians to associate certainly end where these freedoms' rights begin. These free license right do not permit or licenses particular business merchants (that is what nomadic cow rearers are) to carry deadly AK-47 riffles and maim and kill other innocent Nigerians in their homes, rape their mothers, wives and daughters in their houses. Such must be evil freedoms and rights. Nigerians of a particular ethnic group do not have any right to freely graze their cattle on other people's lands and thereby destroy their farm produce. It is this archaic sectional and nepotism mindset that has made Buhari bring Nigeria down to her knees and to a despicable state of nadir where she now wobbles, fumbles and tumbles. Have you ever heard any Southerner complain about all the currency changers and Bureau de Change (BDCs) across every nook and cranny of Nigeria, even though everyone knows that over 95% of the business is controlled by Northerners? No! Do you know why? Because they are not violent. They ply their trade peacefully, even if illegally and illegitimately. By the way, have you ever touched of any of these special breeds of Nigerians? I have personally never heard. This is because we live in a country that is governed by two different sets of laws- one for the highly revered Northerners; the other for the highly despised Southerners. No Nation grows that way. The last time I checked, the freedom of movement guaranteed for Nigerians is not sacrosanct as it can be derogated from by the clear provisions of section 45, through the enactment of a law that is "reasonably justifiable in a democratic society in the interest of defense, public safety, public order, public morality or public health"; or for "the purpose of protecting the rights and freedom of other persons". The last time I checked also, section 41 of the same Constitution is meant for full-blooded human beings; not cows, goats and sheep. That is why section 41 of the Constitution starts by saying

"every citizen of Nigeria is entitled to move freely throughout Nigeria and to reside in any part thereof....". *'Citizen' is defined as "an inhabitant of a particular town or city"; "a person who is at home in any country"; "one entitled to the rights and privileges of a freeman". Other synonyms of citizen are civilian, national, inhabitant resident, voter, settler and dweller. I checked very painstakingly and carefully, using different dictionaries, thesaurus, Black Law's Dictionary and even Wikipedia, but I couldn't and didn't see where cows, goats and sheep were mentioned or regarded as 'citizens' of Nigeria or elsewhere. The Constitution that gives the freedom of movement to "every citizen of Nigeria' also didn't provide that such a citizen must be accompanied by cows, goats and sheep before he can exercise it. So, where is the Buhari Government getting its vibes from? I do not know. Or, do you? Fellow Nigerians, the last time I checked also, we have not been told that Buhari has successfully moved the NASS to amend and alter our country's name, FEDERAL REPUBLIC OF NIGERIA, to the FULANI REPUBLIC OF NIGERIA, or NIGERIAN REPUBLIC OF THE FULANIS, or FULANISED REPUBLIC OF NIGERIA, or THE REPUBLIC OF FULANIS, or FEDERAL REPUBLIC OF THE NORTH, or NORTHERN REPUBLIC, or FEDERAL REPUBLIC OF NORTHERN NIGERIA, or the REPUBLIC OF NORTHERN NIGERIA, or the NORTHERN NIGERIAN REPUBLIC, or the REPUBLIC OF NORTHERN NIGERIA AND OTHER TERRITORIES, or the ISLAMIC REPUBLIC OF NIGERIA, or FEDERATION OF ISLAM AND OTHERS. So, what is going on here? I can no longer understand. Or can you? Nigeria, we hail thee.*

My Comments

Goof? My Senior Advocate, he did not goof. It is in line with his objectives. The President does not believe in Nigeria but the Fulani. If he could, he would have since renamed the country to reflect his illusion that we are conquered territory of the Fulani. It pains him that Lord Lugard did not so name the country and write in the constitution that only the Fulani should rule the country, and with iron hand. He has often said that he has no regret practicing tribalism in governance. What else do we want to hear from him? So, he did not goof. If he has the opportunities, he would do it again and again.

---

9. *EXTRACT FROM THE STATEMENT OF THE NORTHERN ELDERS FORUM (25-5-21)*

'The negative attitude of the Presidency towards engaging Nigerians to tap into ideas, grievances and goodwill of many citizens who mean well is ill informed and, under our current circumstances, dangerous....The forum supports a citizen driven national dialogue and a campaign to get the government to accord its outcome the respect it deserves. The forum extends its hands to groups that genuinely believe that Nigerians should demand and design the type of country we want, and should not wait for people we elected to set the boundaries and conditions of our existence.'

My Comment

The above has been the best part of the Northern Elder Forum's statement. I hope the Southern Elders Forum (SEF), not just the Yoruba Elders Forum (YEF), will come together to robustly respond to the statement of the NEF, in a didactic, civil and elegant manner. Not a word was said by the NEF about the roots of the crisis; skewed and exploitative unitary system. They did not speak on the invasion of the southern forests by the Fulani herdsmen, the destruction of farms and communities, the killings and rapes of women in southern Nigeria. They did not only cherry-pick on issues to address but tried to play on the intelligence of southern Nigerians, only offering halfhearted support for a national dialogue. We love the size and potentials of Nigeria but for Nigeria to move from mere potentials to actual prosperity, we must unclog the wheels of progress. Our agreement to run a true federal structure (of each federating unit) will develop our human and natural resources to build our economy. The progress of each component parts translates to the progress of the nation. Weaker sub-nationals would be supported to grow by the central government while the strong will be given incentives to be stronger and support the weak. That is how to live together in harmony. That is how federalism works! We must transit from this quasi federalism to a true federal system!

However, this statement further goes to show that not the north but the likes of the President are the problems of Nigeria. He will call these fellows infidels and cowards who are backing off at a tough time, who are not true northerners. He would not even mind them. They are simply agents of the south like Yar'dua and even Atiku.

10. Open Letter to President Muhammadu Buhari

Dear President Buhari,

It is with great pain but with deep concern as a fellow human being and your age mate that I send you this private/public letter in the hope that you would be allowed to read it.

I am in pain because the country that Allah has placed on your laps to nurture and protect has virtually slipped out of your hand and is heading to ruins and destruction. Every index that makes a country laid claim to development, survival, safety and security, unity and understanding, and justice and equity has taken a flight under your watch.

You probably are not aware that the country called Nigeria is already up in flames. You may not be aware that you are being used by a clique of very powerful, egocentric and extremely wicked people for their selfish purposes and invidious agenda. And because the position at the top of the pyramid is usually lonely, lonesome, and inaccessible, it has been very difficult for you to know and feel what is going on down below. Those who are guarding the pyramid have made it extremely difficult for well-meaning individuals to have access to you or avail you a second opinion on several issues of state and statecraft.

Worse still, you are afflicted with serious health challenges as evident in the video clips of your brief appearances. You know that you are not well and this is why you have had to be confined to a hospital bed abroad for weeks and months on several occasions. Some of your ailments may not even be clear to you. You have been diagnosed, as reported, with dementia and Alzheimer; these are conditions that sufferers may not be adequately conscious of. But there is no big deal about being ill or having health challenges; most people, if not all, of our age, suffer one major health challenge or the other. It is only our reaction and management of these challenges that differ from one individual to the other.

You have been, to put it bluntly, rendered a glorified but pitiable prisoner as a result of the aforementioned. Those who are using your office for their own selfish advantage have taken full possession of you and have unfortunately blinded you to the realities on the ground. Many atrocious and brutish atrocities are routinely committed in your name because they are fully aware that they would never be held accountable and that the buck stops at your table.

You have been literally handcuffed and manacled as a result of your situation and the only option open to you is to cry out to be released from the prison in which you are. Your entire personal staff cannot help you because they are afraid of the superior officers/officials who are wielding the awesome powers of state hijacked from you. Even state governors are often bullied in your name.

Your ministers and other career politicians will rather die in office than have your current position terminated because your office is their mainstay and breadwinner. All the powers and privileges they currently enjoy and parade are at your behest. If for any reason you leave office today, they know their fish will be out of water.

And yet Nigeria is bleeding. Nigerians are wallowing in unprecedented poverty, want, unemployment, crass nepotism, arrogant and condescending impunity, humongous corruption, humongous debt, alarming insecurity, worrisome absence of safety, confusion and hopelessness.

In the meantime, Nigerians everywhere are all crying out to you to rescue the ship of state whereas you yourself need to be rescued and rescued fast from the clique that holds you by the jugular.

My hope and prayer are that your bold, brilliant and beautiful wife will summon the courage to read this letter to you. Or at least one or two of your children will let this letter reach you. They certainly are aware of your health challenges. They know that several of the do-gooders who are allowed on rare occasions to see you for photo ups hide the truth from the public. They must know too that those on such rare occasions who are allowed to see you say unpalatable things behind your back.

In the name of Almighty Allah, the Most Benevolent, the Most merciful, let people of a good conscience, led by your wife and children urgently release you from the world's most guarded prison and take you back to Daura for needed rest and fresh air, or better still, take you to Germany or the UK for critical medical attention and total rest. That is all you need at this stage of your life, sir.

You have had a distinguished career as a soldier, officer, and Military Head of state. Allah has been most kind and generous to you. Please do not allow those who are embarking on ruinous paths to donate an unenviable epitaph to you.

No nationality in this 21st century can subjugate about 300 other nationalities in Nigeria. The once upon a time Great Britain is sliding to become ordinary England once Scotland and Wales regain their independence and Northern Ireland reunites with its southern kith and kin.

And Saudi Arabia, with all its petro-dollar and United States awesome firepower, has not been able to subjugate tiny Yemen.

Let the message sink.

With esteemed personal regards.

Akogun Tola Adeniyi,
former Managing Director,
The Tribune Newspaper

My Comment

You speak as if the President has made the healthcare facilities available for his own health at retirement. The more reason he would never leave office, if it were by choice. Even if his family members steal all the money, how much would it amount to at retirement to enable him patronize technology in his health stock production in London at every interval? Do you think any of the members of his cabal would donate to his health stock upon leaving the office as you suggest? Do you realize that he would have been long forgotten without this presidency? So, telling him to go and rest is something funny; it is exactly telling him to go and die.

---

11. More Knocks From Nigerians For Remi Tinubu Over 'Reckless' Comments

Tinubu had tackled Adeyemi, her All Progressives Congress's colleague from Kogi West, over the latter's comment on Nigeria's security challenges.

- Saharareporters, New York Apr 28, 2021

A cross-section of Nigerians has criticized the Senator representing Lagos Central District, Remi Tinubu, for tackling her colleague, Smart Adeyemi, who raised pertinent questions about the growing insecurity, and for her playing politics with the lives of Nigerians who are being killed.

Some Nigerians on social media, Twitter, lambasted Tinubu for bringing party affiliations into insecurity, a national disaster consuming lives daily, even as they vowed that the female senator would never emerge as the First Lady in the country.

Tinubu had tackled Adeyemi, her All Progressives Congress's colleague from Kogi West, over the latter's comment on Nigeria's security challenges.

Adeyemi on Tuesday had said the country was facing the worst instability since the civil war.

"This is the worst instability we are facing. In fact, this is worse than the civil war," he said.

But Tinubu interrupting him, had asked, "Are you in PDP (Peoples Democratic Party)? Are you a wolf in sheep's clothing?"

Adeyemi, however, ignored her comments and continued, "We cannot pretend that we are capable of handling the situation in our hands. America, as powerful as they are, when the pandemic came, it came to a point China came to their rescue.

"We shouldn't pretend that we need foreign support now. Billions of naira have been voted for security services and nothing is coming out of it. I'm a party man and I'm supporting APC but it has gotten to a point that as supporters we cannot keep quiet."

Some Comments on Twitter From Angry Readers,

"Ayemojubar @Ayemojubar Said: "Remi Tinubu will Never be a First Lady In Nigeria."

Unu Amaro Kam Siri Kwado @AfamDeluxo wrote: "Imagine if Remi Tinubu becomes first lady, omo, some of us will be chased away from planet earth. A tall horrible woman. A bigot. A cretin. The same woman that bashed Ndiigbo during the last election."

Ifa Funsho @funshographix, "Remi Tinubu is not preparing to be first lady. She just doesn't have sense. The name Nigeria will not even exist before 2023. Smart Adeyemi is already linking the information of everyone should go their separate ways. Nigeria will divide before 2023."

Also, @theonly1acre says, Remi Tinubu wants to be the First Lady at the expense of the drop of blood of innocent Nigerians. May that dream never come true."

Another Nigerian said, "Tinubu and his wife's ambition to become the President and the First Lady supersede every calamity that is currently befalling this country. But truthfully, they are not my problem. My major problem is the Nigerian youth who, just as our old generation of politicians/leaders has failed to position the country on the path to greatness, has also failed to collectively get it right in choosing worthy leaders for the country.

"There needs to be a break from the norm in future elections. The French youths did it with Emmanuel Macron. We can do it!"

Another commentator wrote, "And who voted for her husband to become president?? These people ehn, they don't even know if Nigeria will exist in 2023 or if they will be alive and they are already fighting on who should be the First Lady......I am a Yoruba guy but I have always believed we the South-West contributed to the declining state of this country, all thanks to godfatherism we cherish so much."

My Comments

Sen. Adeyemi was brought in by the All Progress Congress led by Sen. Tinubu, the husband of Remi, to remove Sen. Dino Malaye, a bone in the neck of the President The election probably favoured him because Dino must lose at all cost. So, he was not expected by the clique Sen. Remi Tinubu belongs to criticize the President's administration, instead, he should continue to sing its praises. He had actually lived up to that expectation for a long time, but being who he is, he could not sustain the silence for too long. Sen. Remi Tinubu, knowing how he came to the senate, was angered. She wanted Sen. Adeyemi to be loyal to the government instead of the nation, just as they have held the South West region to ransom. However, her impatience was what Sen. Adeyemi needed to be popular again if he could throw away the long spoon with which he had eaten with the devil. I can assure you that it is not easy; they would caution him and remind him of the many tales and we would no long hear from him. Even for this he has already done, he would serve the accompanied punishment for a long time. He has already joined them. He is already in it.

Index

Abuja, 15, 174
Africa, 13, 29, 64, 77, 78, 87,
    92, 103, 104, 114, 117,
    118, 123, 128, 132, 134,
    135, 136, 155, 156, 157,
    165, 167, 171, 174, 186,
    211
African, 16, 58, 63, 66, 70, 79,
    134, 135, 155, 166, 168,
    169, 183
Allah, 7, 69, 75, 112, 114,
    116, 119, 198, 200
Almighty God, 8, 17, 28
America, 10, 24, 53, 68, 90,
    91, 102, 103, 118, 148,
    150, 154, 155, 156, 157,
    190, 202
Apostle Paul, 9, 28, 91
Assurances, 28
*Attorney General of the
    Federation*, 11, 12, 31, 110
Baba Bubu, xiii, 2, 3, 4, 5, 6,
    7, 8, 9, 10, 11, 12, 13, 14,
    16, 17, 20, 23, 30, 31, 39,
    40, 59, 61, 62, 64, 66, 67,
    68, 69, 70, 71, 72, 73, 74,
    76, 78, 80, 85, 89, 90, 93,
    94, 98, 99, 101, 103, 104,
    106, 107, 108, 109, 111,
    112, 113, 114, 118, 119,
    120, 121, 122, 123, 124,
    125, 127, 128, 129, 130,
    132, 135, 137, 139, 145,
    148, 151, 153, 157, 158

Baba Obasara, 30, 61, 79, 84,
    93, 149
bankers, 39, 42
Benue State, 9, 187, 193
bigot, 17, 70, 72, 75, 110, 203
Bubuism, 5, 8
Catholic Church, 1, 8, 44, 50,
    51, 101, 168
Christian Churches, 12
Christian life, 1, 50
Churches, 17
*Corporate Affairs
    Commission*, 12
Corruption, 110
David Oyedepo, xi, 12
economy, viii, 13, 29, 38, 39,
    40, 42, 53, 78, 80, 81, 82,
    83, 84, 85, 86, 87, 88, 91,
    92, 93, 107, 128, 149, 158,
    164, 166, 174, 175, 197
Education, 13, 19, 110
Ejike Mbaka, 9, 162
Enyinnaya Abaribe, xi, 11, 27
Esan, 17, 21, 58, 61, 64, 98
Federal Soldiers, 7
Fulani bandits, 10
Fulani friends, 2
Gloominess, 7
*Golden Rule of
    Accumulations*, 28
Goodluck Jonathan, 14, 25,
    181

Government, 12, 13, 15, 38, 123, 160, 166, 167, 168, 169, 191, 192
Governor, 164
Grassed, 3
Hausa-Fulani language, 12
Health, viii, 136, 148, 150
Henry Aigbe Igberaese, 6
Humanism, 19
Igbo infidel, 10
indigent students, 19
injustice and oppression, 12
inner selves, 8
innocent blood, 4
Israel, xiii, 59
Jean-Baptiste Colbert, ix, 39
Joseph's brothers, 8
Kano State, 15, 187
Keynes, ix, 35, 36, 37, 38
Lagos State, 12, 15, 188
lamentations, ix, 8
larceny, 22
Local Governments Areas, 13
maternal complications, 20
Matthew Hassan Kukah, xi, 9, 12, 100
Mau Mau Movements, 8
medical tourism, 21, 77, 122, 152
Memoranda of Understanding, 25
middle belt, 173, 174
Middle East, 5
middlemen, 4
military, 23, 61, 63, 64, 65, 91, 93, 167, 178

Minister of Justice, 11, 12, 31
Mosques, 17
my tormentors, 8
Myrdal, 16
National Army Academy, 10
National Honour, 12
national outputs, 19
national pledge, 16
nepotism, 12, 29, 194, 199
nervous systems, 28
Nigeria, vii, viii, ix, xi, xii, 1, 3, 5, 6, 7, 8, 10, 12, 13, 14, 21, 22, 29, 30, 31, 35, 41, 54, 60, 61, 62, 63, 65, 67, 68, 69, 71, 73, 75, 76, 78, 79, 80, 81, 83, 84, 85, 92, 99, 101, 103, 104, 107, 108, 114, 121, 122, 124, 126, 127, 128, 129, 131, 132, 142, 143, 149, 150, 155, 156, 157, 160, 161, 164, 165, 166, 167, 168, 170, 171, 172, 173, 174, 176, 177, 179, 180, 181, 182, 183, 184, 185, 186, 190, 191, 193, 196, 197, 198, 199, 200, 201, 202, 203, 204
Nnamdi Kanu, xi, 11, 12, 69, 184
Noble Prize, 12
northerners, 12, 15, 16, 73, 122, 197
Nyesom Wike, xi, 11
Obliviousness, 8
Odumegu Ojukwu, 6

Office, 36, 115
Ogun State, 188
oligarchy, 26
Olusegun Obasanjo, 13, 30, 161, 173
orthodox models, 20
Out-of-Pocket model, 20, 143, 144, 145, 147
Paranoia, 1
Patriotism, 11
Personality, 22
philosophers, 22, 23, 44, 46, 48, 88, 94
Police, 110, 193
politics, 3, 22, 29, 36, 85, 99, 120, 166, 167, 190, 202
power, xi, xii, 3, 23, 27, 28, 32, 33, 41, 60, 62, 63, 64, 65, 66, 70, 71, 72, 77, 80, 98, 101, 103, 108, 115, 118, 119, 120, 126, 129, 164, 165, 167, 170, 174, 175, 178, 182, 192
premature deaths, 7
presidential palace, 21
production, 20, 90, 135, 139, 151, 190, 201
ransom, 23, 100, 106, 166, 168, 184, 204
ransoms, 3
regions and religion, 6
revered army, 3
Revolution, xi, 27

Robert Solow's Model, 28
Sectionalism, 13
Security, 110, 176, 192
Sergius Ogun, 21
Shehu Usman Aliyu Shagari, 16
sickness fund, 20, 149
Society, 36, 135
southern, 6, 10, 15, 26, 73, 167, 197, 200
spread effect, 16
St. Thomas Aquinas, ix, 43
Structuralism, 24
suicide rate, 7
taxation, 22
technology, 20, 151, 176, 190, 201
terrorists, 3, 4, 10, 12, 63, 67, 103, 104, 105
Thomism, 43, 44, 45, 48, 50, 51, 52
Umaru Musa Yar'dua, 16
United Kingdom, 20, 66, 150, 152, 184, 190
Upper and Lower Chambers, 21
Vice Chancellors, 27
war crime, 5
wasteful consumption, 20
widespread poverty, 15
Wole Soyinka, xi, 12, 68, 162
youth-adult life, 2

The Author

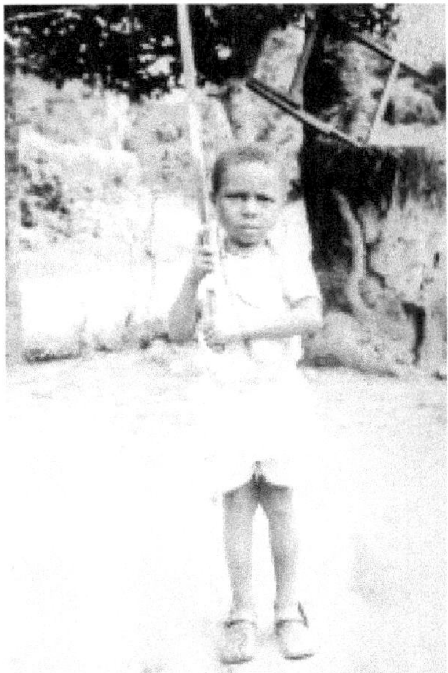

Ilenloa Igberaese hails from Eror-Uromi, Edo State. He holds the Ph.D. in Economics of the University of Benin and a Senior Lecturer in Mudiame University, Irua. His numerous academic publications on the Nigeria and Africa problems are spread in local and international journals/conference proceedings. He has also been the Guest Lecturer and Speaker in many conferences and notable events across the world, winning the best track presentation award in an ITAC conference held in University of London in 2012.

Dr. Igberaese is the Secretary of the Edo State Chapter of the Nigerian Economic Society and the Representative of State Chairmen in the South-South zone of the professional society. He is also the founder and president of Edo Policy Round Table.

He is happily married to Tina, and blessed with five children.

His other books are:

- Poetry for schools
- Our fathers are dead
- Too decent for marriage
- When the gods are angry – A play of Political Satire
- The anti-christs are here
- No water at home
- African fable of the wise
- The new coven – yet to be published.